ALLIANCE OF NEPTUNE AND PAN

UNION OF ERIE WITH THE ATLANTIC

The ERIE CANAL

by MARTHA E. KENDALL

NATIONAL GEOGRAPHIC
Washington, D.C.

THIS BOOK IS DEDICATED TO MY HUSBAND JOE, MY CO-CAPTAIN
ON THE ERIE CANAL AND IN LIFE, AND TO OUR WORLD-CLASS CREW,
OUR CHILDREN, JEFF AND KATIE. — MEK

The author would like to acknowledge the following for their help along the way: Andrew Kitzmann
of the Erie Canal Museum; the MacDonald family of Canal Princess Charters; Judy Bennett; Julie
and Jocko Cleland; Jack and Evie Frohm; the Humphrey family; Chuck and Cynthia Kendall; Bernie
Lehman; Doug and Pam Meier; Captain Bob and June Schleicher; Lynn and Ron Ward; Mac and Betsy
Warner; and the late Dr. Marvin A. Rapp who taught that "history begins in your own backyard."

The publisher also thanks Andrew Kitzmann of the Erie Canal Museum
for his expert review of this book.

PUBLISHED BY THE NATIONAL GEOGRAPHIC SOCIETY
John M. Fahey, Jr., *President and Chief Executive Officer*
Gilbert M. Grosvenor, *Chairman of the Board*
Nina D. Hoffman, *Executive Vice President; President, Book Publishing Group*

PREPARED BY THE BOOK DIVISION
Nancy Laties Feresten, *Vice President, Editor-in-Chief, Children's Books*
Bea Jackson, *Director of Design and Illustrations, Children's Books*
Carl Mehler, *Director of Maps*

STAFF FOR THIS BOOK
Marfé Ferguson Delano, Jennifer Emmett, *Editors*
David M. Seager, *Art Director*
Lori Epstein, Charlotte Fullerton, *Illustrations Editors*
Rebecca Baines, *Editorial Assistant*
Rachel Armor, *Editorial Intern*
Justin Morrill, The M Factory, Inc.; Matt Chwastyk; Michael McNey,
Map Research, Design, and Production
Ruth Thompson, *Production Designer*
Jennifer A. Thornton, *Managing Editor*
Gary Colbert, *Production Director*
Lewis R. Bassford, *Production Manager*
Susan Borke, *Legal and Business Affairs*
Nicole Elliott, Maryclare Tracy, *Manufacturing Managers*

LIBRARY OF CONGRESS CATALOGING-IN-PUBLICATION INFORMATION
Kendall, Martha E., 1947-
The Erie Canal / by Martha E. Kendall.
p. cm.
ISBN 978-1-4263-0022-6 (trade) — ISBN 978-1-4263-0023-3 (library)
1. Erie Canal (N.Y.) — History — Juvenile literature. I. Title.
HE396.E6K46 2005
386'.48'09747 — dc22
2007029386

Printed in the United States of America

CONTENTS

Chapter One

HIGH SPEED!

PEOPLE SAID, "YOU CAN'T MAKE WATER RUN uphill." They thought it would be impossible to build a canal across mountains and through wilderness. But DeWitt Clinton, governor of New York State, proved them wrong. In 1825, he celebrated the completion of the Eighth Wonder of the World. It was called the Erie Canal, and it changed America forever.

This manmade waterway, 363 miles long, stretched from Albany, New York, an eastern city, across the Appalachian Mountains to Buffalo, New York, at that time considered a western city.

The Erie Canal made travel easier, cheaper, and faster than ever before between the American East and West. It is hard for us to imagine that transportation on the canal

CELEBRATING THE OPENING OF THE ERIE CANAL IN 1825

at four miles per hour could be considered "high speed," but in the 1820s, that pace seemed very fast indeed. Two hundred years ago, the canal—only four feet deep and 40 feet wide—was a miracle of technology. By means of 83 locks, the waterway climbed an elevation of 675 feet as it crossed the hills and valleys of New York State.

Before the canal was built, travelers between Albany and Buffalo endured the trip in bone-rattling, horse-drawn wagons that bounced over rough roads often compared to corduroy, a fabric with ridges. Because getting stuck in the mud was a common problem, logs were laid down, side by side, on top of the dirt. Wagons moved slowly as the wheels

TRAVELING BY COACH IN THE EARLY 1800s WAS SLOW, UNCOMFORTABLE, AND UNRELIABLE BECAUSE OF THE TERRIBLE ROAD CONDITIONS.

THE COHOES FALLS ON THE MOHAWK RIVER. WATERFALLS, ROCKS, AND RAPIDS MADE TRAVEL ON THE MIGHTY MOHAWK RIVER ALMOST ALWAYS DIFFICULT AND OFTEN IMPOSSIBLE.

slammed over timbers that must have felt like perpetual speed bumps. Taking a trip on one of these roads was called "hitting the logs." With good weather, good luck, and no breakdowns, an eight-horse freight wagon hitting the logs could make the journey in 15 days. But if conditions were bad, the trip might take six weeks.

Instead of making the whole trip on land, some people covered part of the distance in small boats that were poled, pulled, or paddled up wild rivers. The largest of these, the Mohawk River, was dangerous when high, impassable when low. Rapids, waterfalls, and areas choked with rocks made

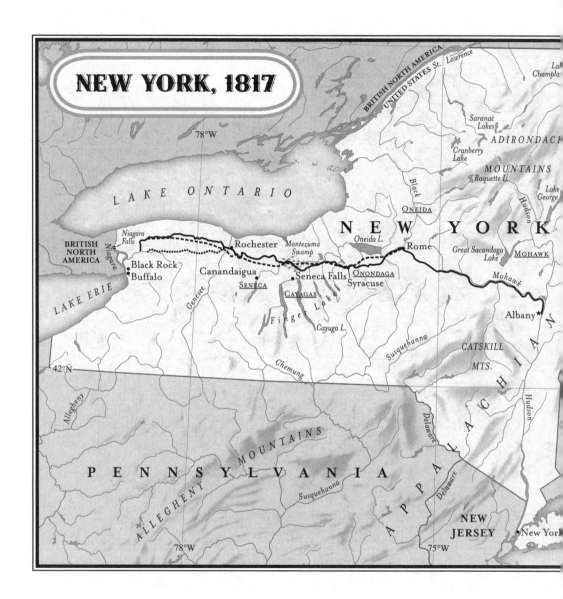

NEW YORK, 1817

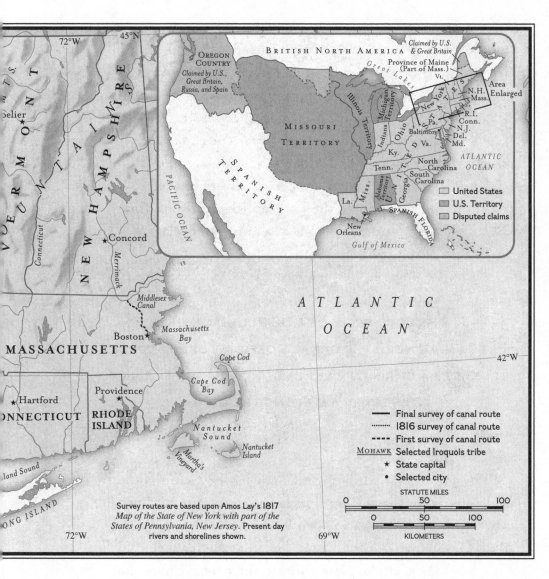

PROPOSED ROUTES FOR THE ERIE CANAL HAD TO DEAL
WITH CHALLENGES OF CROSSING RUGGED TERRAIN BETWEEN
BUFFALO IN THE WEST AND ALBANY IN THE EAST.

some stretches of it unpassable at any time of year. Goods had to be loaded into wagons and hauled around these sections of the river. The process was slow, dangerous, and expensive.

Before the canal opened, farmers paid a hundred dollars per ton to transport their sacks of flour from western New York State to Albany by road. After the canal opened, travel between Buffalo and Albany by water would take barely a week. Then only two more days were needed to travel the 162 miles down the Hudson River to New York City. The cost would drop from one hundred dollars to ten dollars a ton.

THE LOUD BOOM OF A 32-POUND CANNON ANNOUNCED THE CANAL'S OFFICIAL OPENING. IT SET OFF A CHAIN OF CANNONS THUNDERING THE NEWS TO EVERY TOWN ALONG THE CANAL.

The completion of the Erie Canal caused so much excitement that the celebrations lasted for a month. They officially began at 9:00 a.m. on Wednesday, October 26, 1825. Governor DeWitt Clinton led a parade from the courthouse in Buffalo, New York, to the canal. There, he and James Tallmadge Jr., the state's lieutenant governor, boarded their boat, the *Seneca Chief*. Made of wood, it was a long, low packet boat designed to carry passengers. Four gray horses were harnessed to it. The horses pulled the boat as they walked along the towpath next to the canal. Other boats followed behind the *Seneca Chief.*

The loud boom of a 32-pound cannon announced the canal's official opening. It set off a chain of cannons thundering the news to every town along the canal. As each one heard the roar, it fired its own cannon. Towns too small to have a cannon shot off guns instead. It took 81 minutes for the announcement to boom from Buffalo to New York City. This was probably the fastest long-distance news had ever traveled. When the last cannon at the southern end of the New York City harbor responded, the message was returned. The artillery roared its way back to Buffalo, a roundtrip grand salute that some reporters said took three hours and 20 minutes, while others claimed the process took only a little more than two hours. But there was no debate about the most important fact: The Erie Canal had opened!

Chapter Two

WEDDING OF THE WATERS

TWO LARGE BARRELS PAINTED RED, WHITE, and blue stood on the front deck of DeWitt Clinton's boat, the *Seneca Chief*. They contained water from one of the five Great Lakes, Lake Erie. Buffalo is located on its shore. Clinton carried the barrels of water so that he could fulfill a dream he had worked toward for more than 15 years. He planned to pour the fresh water from Lake Erie into the salt water of the Atlantic Ocean when the boat reached the New York City harbor. This ceremony, called the Wedding of the Waters, would represent the new connection between the interior of the United States and the Atlantic. On their way to that ceremony, the *Seneca Chief* and the line of boats behind it paused for celebrations in 20 canal towns, big and small.

ON NOVEMBER 4, 1825, NEW YORK GOVERNOR DEWITT CLINTON POURED WATER FROM LAKE ERIE, IN WHAT WAS THEN THE AMERICAN WEST, INTO THE ATLANTIC OCEAN AT NEW YORK CITY. IN THIS CEREMONY, HE "MARRIED" THE AMERICAN WEST WITH THE COUNTRIES WHOSE SHIPS SAILED THE ATLANTIC.

As the boats neared Rochester, local residents ignored the rain and lined the canal to greet Clinton. A Rochester boat called the *Young Lion of the West* met the *Seneca Chief.*

"Who goes there?" called a man from the *Young Lion.*

"Our brother from the west on the waters of the Great Lakes," answered someone from the governor's boat.

The crowd quieted, straining to hear the voices. "By what means have they come so far?" asked a man on the *Young Lion.*

"By the grand Erie Canal," came the response from the *Seneca Chief.*

"By what authority, and by whom, was such a great piece of work done?" asked the man on the *Young Lion.*

"By the authority and energy of the patriotic people of the state of New York," the man on the *Seneca Chief* replied.

Hundreds of Rochester's citizens must have swelled with pride, for many had helped to build the canal. The construction had already promoted local wealth. In 1815, Rochester had had only 331 human inhabitants. The few people who passed through called it "an emporium of mud." They made fun of the tree stumps left jutting up out of its streets. But in only two years, because the canal was coming, Rochester's population soared. Few of the people who watched the fireworks display to celebrate the canal's opening could have guessed how much more wealth the canal would create. Rochester became the first boomtown in America, transformed from a frontier village to a thriving city because the canal helped it to ship and receive goods and people from all over the world.

Even though the Erie Canal made transportation across the state faster than it had ever been, people were in no hurry to rush the celebrations. When Clinton's parade of boats arrived at a town, crowds cheered, speeches were given, toasts were offered, bands played, couples danced, fireworks exploded, and guns and cannons boomed. Many boats joined the parade, which at times measured five miles long.

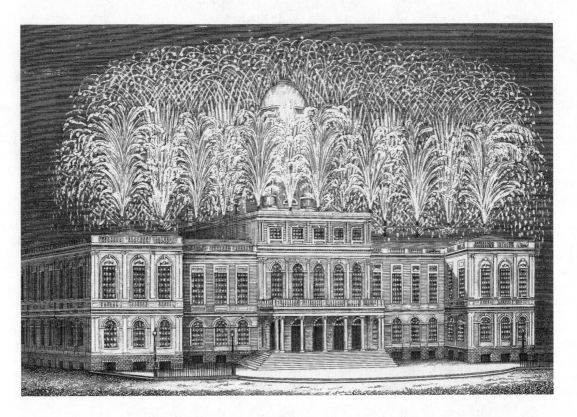

FIREWORKS IN NEW YORK CITY CELEBRATED THE COMPLETION OF THE ERIE CANAL.

IN THIS KEG, DeWITT CLINTON CARRIED FRESH
WATER FROM LAKE ERIE TO POUR INTO THE SALT WATER OF THE
ATLANTIC OCEAN IN THE NEW YORK CITY HARBOR.

Unlike the others, two towns were unhappy about
the opening of the canal. People in Rome, a village on
a small canal, had hoped the Erie would breathe fresh
life into their businesses. But for engineering reasons,
the Erie's route passed a half-mile away from Rome's
downtown. A few angry citizens held a funeral when
the Erie opened. They knew the *Seneca Chief* carried kegs
of Lake Erie water bound for the Atlantic Ocean. In
protest, four men filled a black keg with water from their
old canal and dumped it into the new one. Imitating a
military funeral, soldiers turned the flags around and
muffled the drums. The "mourners" then gave three sad
groans before leaving.

The other town that did not welcome the canal was
Schenectady (sken-EK-ta-dee). It had a thriving hauling
industry. Its horse-drawn wagons carried people and freight
from the Hudson River to a navigable section of the Mohawk
River. The canal would replace the need for their business.

Neither Rome nor Schenectady realized how much
prosperity the Erie would bring them in only a few years.
Like all towns on or near the canal, they ended up thriving
because of the people and products transported on the Erie.

On November 2, after more than a week of celebrations,
Governor Clinton's boat parade arrived in Albany, the

"**A**MERICA CAN NEVER FORGET TO ACKNOWLEDGE
THAT THEY HAVE BUILT THE LONGEST CANAL
IN THE WORLD, IN THE LEAST TIME, WITH THE LEAST
EXPERIENCE, FOR THE LEAST MONEY, AND TO THE
GREATEST PUBLIC BENEFIT."

state capital. Cheering spectators filled the docks, bridges,
and shore. National officials and local leaders gathered in
the State Assembly building. After a chorus and orchestra
performed, the speeches began. Then Clinton and the
other statesmen joined the crowds outside, visited a bridge
whose decorations made it look like a grand old European

church, and finally seated themselves at two long tables that were shaded by a tent and large enough for their banquet of 600 people. After dinner, the entertainment included the reciting of poems and the presentation of a play.

The canal ended in Albany, but Clinton's trip was far from over. One hundred sixty-two miles remained on the Hudson River to New York City. The next morning, amid the applause and cheers of an even larger crowd than the one

BOATS FILLED THE NEW YORK CITY HARBOR
TO CELEBRATE THE OPENING OF THE ERIE CANAL.

that had welcomed Clinton the day before, the boat parade began the final stretch of the journey. The horses and mules that had pulled the boats on the canal were unhitched. The Hudson River was much deeper than the canal, so boats with paddlewheels, powered by steam engines, could be used to pull the canal boats along. After two days on the Hudson, the procession arrived in New York City.

Governor Clinton fulfilled his dream on Friday, November 4, 1825. Forty-six decorated, flag-waving ships escorted the small canal boats into the New York City

harbor. In the Wedding of the Waters, Clinton poured the kegs of Erie water into the Atlantic Ocean. By doing so, he "married" the American West with the countries in Europe, Africa, and South America whose ships crossed the Atlantic. It was a match created by imagination, courage, and hard work.

Describing the canal, one newspaper proclaimed, "Next to the establishment of American Independence, it is the greatest achievement of the age." Building the canal made Americans feel that they and their country could do anything.

While Clinton held the Wedding of the Waters ceremony at sea, a giant parade made its way along the streets of Manhattan in downtown New York City. At one point the parade measured a mile and a half long, the biggest foot parade America had ever seen. A Grand Ball prolonged the festivities into the night.

The celebration was still not over. The *Seneca Chief* turned around and led boats back to Buffalo. There, on November 23, Judge Samuel Wilkeson, a strong supporter of the canal in Buffalo, was given the honor of pouring water from the Atlantic Ocean into Lake Erie.

William Stone, a journalist who witnessed the opening of the canal, wrote, "America can never forget to acknowledge that they have built the longest canal in the world, in the least time, with the least experience, for the least money, and to the greatest public benefit."

Now, almost 200 years later, rare is the New York town or city without a street named for DeWitt Clinton.

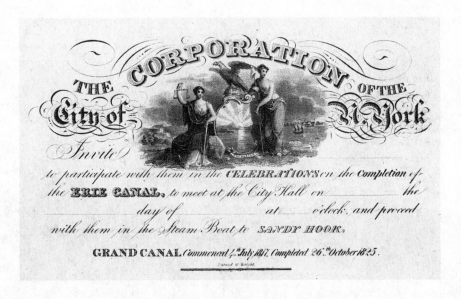

**THE OFFICIAL INVITATION TO THE
CANAL'S OPENING CELEBRATION IN NEW YORK CITY
ON NOVEMBER 4, 1825.**

He won the people's respect when he continued with his revolutionary Erie Canal even when his political enemies made fun of it as "Clinton's Ditch."

How did he dare begin construction of a canal when the undertaking demanded technology beyond anything yet developed? How did he dare risk more money than any public project had ever used in the country's history? And how did the success of his dream open the interior of the young United States?

The answers tell one of America's greatest stories: the building of the Erie Canal.

Chapter Three

SOLUTION FROM A JAIL CELL

JESSE HAWLEY SAID PEOPLE LAUGHED AT him in 1805 when he first suggested building a canal between Lake Erie and the Hudson River. But 20 years later at the opening of that canal, no one was laughing at him. Instead, they were cheering.

Long before Jesse Hawley was born, Native Americans understood the importance of transportation across the rolling hills of what is now central and western New York State. The Indians called their territory the "Land of the Long House," where neighboring peoples lived in peace under one common law. The Seneca, Mohawk, Oneida, Onondaga, and Cayuga were united in an alliance known as the Iroquois Confederacy.

About 15 miles south of the route the canal would follow,

IROQUOIS INDIANS LIVED IN "LONG HOUSES" AND DEVELOPED A NETWORK OF TRAILS NEAR THE ROUTE THE ERIE CANAL WOULD ONE DAY FOLLOW.

the Iroquois cleared their Great Central Trail, a 12- to 18-inch-wide path through the forest. Using this trail, which connected their principal villages, fast runners carried messages that sometimes traveled as much as one hundred miles in a day. From the Great Central Trail, a network of smaller trails and waterways fanned out across Iroquois territory.

After the United States won independence from Britain in the Revolutionary War, President George Washington worried that the brand new country might split into two separate nations—one east of the Appalachian Mountains, and another west of them. Just as the Iroquois had recognized the importance of communication to unify their nation, Washington believed that people and products in the newly established United States needed to be able to go back and forth easily between the two parts of the young country. A canal could provide the means for them to do that, but during Washington's lifetime, constructing a canal across a mountain range would take manpower, money, and technology way beyond anything then known.

In 1792 the New York State Senate created the Northern and Western Inland Lock and Navigation Companies. They built a few small canals and locks, but the projects were not profitable because the costs of construction were so high. Neither the government nor private companies were ready to begin a large, coordinated canal project.

During the American Revolution, statesman Gouverneur Morris had expressed interest in the idea of a

GOUVERNEUR MORRIS ("GOUVERNEUR" WAS HIS FIRST NAME) WAS AN EARLY SUPPORTER OF THE IDEA OF BUILDING A CANAL TO LINK THE EAST AND THE WEST. HE LOST HIS LEG IN A CARRIAGE ACCIDENT.

water connection between the Hudson River and the Great Lakes, or as he called them, the "great western seas." After the war, as one of the authors of the U.S. Constitution, he thought of the United States as one unified nation, not just a collection of separate states. What better way to unify the country than to create an easy means of transportation linking its states? He held onto that idea for many years, and in 1803 he wrote the surveyor-general of New York about creating "an artificial river" from Lake Erie to the Hudson. He predicted these waters would open the West. "As yet," he wrote, "we only crawl along the outer shell of our country. The interior excels the part we inhabit in soil, in climate, in everything. The proudest empire in Europe is but a bubble compared to what America will be, must be, in the course of two centuries, perhaps one."

Morris thought a canal and its benefits might be achieved in one or two hundred years. But Jesse Hawley believed the canal could be built right away.

Hawley, a merchant, promoted his idea for a canal from a very unlikely spot—a jail cell. His business had gone broke because of the high cost of hauling flour and wheat from farms in the Genesee Valley of western New York state to New York City. The terrible roads—dusty and bumpy in summer, muddy and rutted in winter—made transportation take a long time and cost a great deal. To avoid being thrown into debtors' prison because he could not pay his bills, Hawley fled to Pennsylvania. However, he could not flee his guilty conscience. He returned to New York State to serve his time, 20 months in a jail in the village of Canandaigua (can-an-DAY-gwa).

In his cell, Hawley wrote 14 detailed articles about his idea for a canal linking the Hudson River and Lake Erie. The articles were printed as a series in 1807 and 1808 in the local newspaper, the *Ontario Messenger*. Hawley described canals in France and England, and he outlined a route for a canal across New York State. He estimated such a canal could be built for six million dollars (about one hundred million dollars today). The series was soon printed in newspapers across the country. Some readers called Hawley a "maniac," but one person impressed by his ideas was DeWitt Clinton, at that time the popular mayor of New York City.

Clinton wanted to find out more. In 1810 the state legislature appointed him to the first Board of Canal Commissioners, five men eager to study the possibility of implementing Hawley's plan. They traveled the proposed route and made extensive notes about what they saw— abundant wildlife, hills, rivers, and wilderness. Clinton

"IF THE CANAL IS TO BE A SHOWER OF GOLD, IT WILL FALL UPON NEW YORK; IF A RIVER OF GOLD, IT WILL FLOW INTO HER LAP."

believed building a canal would be possible, and he wanted to make it happen. However, the War of 1812 against Great Britain took the state's attention away.

When the war against England ended in 1815, Clinton once again began promoting the idea of building a canal as Hawley had described it. All across the state, it became a topic of daily debate. People against the idea pointed out that canals should connect two important things. The proposed Erie Canal, they said, would connect New York

City with little more than wilderness. After all, on the shore of Lake Erie, Buffalo and its neighboring town, Black Rock, together had only 700 residents. Also, skeptics noted that the 27-mile Middlesex Canal between Boston and the Merrimack River was the longest canal in the United States, and it was losing money. The largest canal in Europe, France's 144-mile Canal du Midi, was less than half as long as the proposed Erie. The Erie would stretch 363 miles and climb elevations totaling 675 feet. Critics called the idea "Clinton's Folly." One man said the notion of building a canal all the way across New York State seemed as absurd as "the possibility of a canal to the moon."

Even if the canal could be constructed, how would such

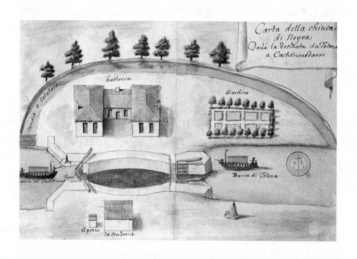

A LOCK ON THE CANAL DU MIDI IN FRANCE.
THIS CANAL WAS THE LONGEST ONE IN EUROPE. THE PROPOSED ERIE CANAL
WOULD STRETCH MORE THAN TWICE AS FAR.

a huge undertaking be paid for? At that time, a public works project costing six million dollars was unheard of. Former President Thomas Jefferson called the proposal "madness." James Madison, who had succeeded Jefferson as President in 1809, agreed that the project was impossible and declared that he would not provide any federal money.

But many liked the idea. A New York State assemblyman who supported Clinton and the canal said, "If the canal is to be a shower of gold, it will fall upon New York; if a river of gold, it will flow into her lap." The citizens of the state agreed with him. In 1817 Clinton ran for governor. Voting for him meant voting for the canal. He was elected in the biggest landslide in state history: 43,310 votes to 1,479.

The state legislature passed the Canal Bill on April 15, 1817, but the Legislative Council of Revision could still cancel it. One man on the council who opposed the canal said that the state needed to save its money to prepare for another war against England, which he said would happen within two years. Angrily, another man stood and declared, "If we must choose between the canal and war, I am in favor of the canal!" The Erie Canal Bill passed the council, by just one vote.

Three days after DeWitt Clinton took office as governor, America's greatest construction project was begun. On the Fourth of July, 1817, near Rome, New York, the final speaker at the groundbreaking ceremony proclaimed, "Let us proceed with the work."

And the digging began.

Chapter Four

DIGGING CLINTON'S DITCH

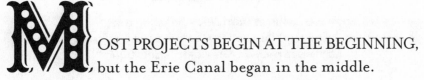

MOST PROJECTS BEGIN AT THE BEGINNING, but the Erie Canal began in the middle.

It made sense to start with the easiest section, a remote stretch of flat land between the town of Rome in the east and Seneca Falls to the west. Everyone involved would learn as the construction progressed, and the new knowledge could be applied in the more difficult parts. Clinton and the other canal commissioners knew that inexperience was one of their biggest weaknesses, so starting with a relatively simple section would give the best chance of early success.

If the canal were begun at either end, builders would immediately need to cut through rocks and construct locks—two challenges they felt far from ready to tackle. They feared that any early failures might cause the project to be canceled.

BEFORE CANAL BUILDING COULD BEGIN, WORKERS FIRST HAD TO CUT A PATH FOR IT 60 FEET WIDE THROUGH THE WILDERNESS OF CENTRAL AND WESTERN NEW YORK STATE.

**BENJAMIN WRIGHT, WHO OVERSAW THE
CONSTRUCTION OF THE FIRST SECTION OF THE CANAL, BECAME KNOWN
AS "THE FATHER OF AMERICAN ENGINEERING."**

They also worried that a canal begun in Albany might never reach all the way to Lake Erie. So, construction started in the middle, working both ways at once.

The canal commissioners chose Benjamin Wright to supervise construction of the first section, about 73 miles long. He and James Geddes had already surveyed the route, measuring the land's ups and downs and plotting the canal's exact path. Both of them were judges, not professional surveyors, but they had learned how to survey when settling legal disputes about property lines. Neither of them was a professional engineer, either. In fact, there were no trained engineers in the United States at this time. But Wright and Geddes, like others involved in the canal project, got on-the-job training.

The finished ditch had to measure four feet deep and 40 feet across at the top, sloping to 28 feet wide at the bottom.

Because the canal would be too narrow for boats powered by sails and too shallow for steamboats with paddlewheels, a towpath ten feet wide was leveled along one side of it. Horses or mules would walk the towpath, pulling the boats behind them.

To make room for the canal and the towpath next to it, workers had to cut a path 60 feet wide through a wilderness of massive, towering trees. As Wright's son noted when he helped his father map where the canal would go, "he could count upon the fingers of one hand" the few spots of ground being farmed along this route. This was mostly virgin forest, never cut before. The trees soared upward into the sky, some with straight trunks whose lowest branches were 40 to 50 feet off the ground. The uneven forest floor was packed with fallen trees, branches, bark, mushrooms, mosses, ferns, and decaying leaves. Who could clear this dense wilderness, and how could it be done?

As for the "who," farmers who lived near the route were hired as contractors because they knew the land and people of the area. Their role was to get workers, equipment, horses, and oxen for the stretch of the canal they were hired to construct. For the "how," workers developed new tools and strategies to topple the huge trees. The inventors' names are unknown today, but these creative men developed faster ways to cut the timber.

Chopping down a giant tree could require more than a hundred swings of an axe. To speed the job, the workers came up with a simple yet effective strategy. A man would string a cable from the top of a tree to a wheel situated on a spindle on the ground. By cranking the wheel around and thereby shortening the cable length, the worker caused the tree to bend more and more until its trunk broke. The tree stump would remain, jutting up into the air. Its roots still stretched deep into the ground. Another invention was called for—a stump puller. It was a giant contraption consisting of two 16-foot wheels and an axle 30 feet long and 20 inches in diameter. The workers wrapped a cable around a wheel drum mounted midway on the axle between the wheels. They positioned the puller over the stump and wrapped one end of the cable around it. Horses or oxen pulled the cable on the other end. With this machine, which cost about $250, a crew of seven men and four work animals could yank out the stumps and roots of 40 large trees a day.

During the first year's work season in 1817, 1,000 men worked on 58 miles of the canal until winter snow and freezing temperatures called a halt to the effort. Snowfall that winter proved especially heavy, and that, combined with drenching spring rains, left the land too soggy for digging until late May in 1818. That year, the number of men grew to almost 4,000. They and 1,500 horses continued the work begun the year before, and they tackled 15 additional miles, too. They hoped they might complete the entire middle section, all 73 miles, by the end of 1819.

After the land was cleared, the ditch needed to be dug. Instead of digging with shovels and taking the dirt away in

THIS HUGE STUMP PULLER WAS JUST ONE OF MANY INVENTIONS
THAT WORKERS CREATED IN ORDER TO CLEAR THE LAND
IN PREPARATION FOR BUILDING THE ERIE CANAL.

wheelbarrows, workers came up with a more efficient way to get the job done. They harnessed horses to plows they had fitted with cast iron spikes that yanked and pulled the dirt and tangled roots out of the ground.

But these inventions could not be used when the construction crews tried to cross the Montezuma swamps, four and a half miles of mud on the western end of the middle section. The horse-drawn plows that had speeded up the clearing elsewhere were useless here because the horses sank into the soggy muck. Men had to dig by hand, and progress was painfully slow. Calling the marshes the "Digger's Misery" or "Bottomless Pit," the laborers slogged their way along. Men tried to dig while standing in muddy water up to their waists. Leeches clung to their legs, and the

sun burned their shoulders. As soon as a hole was dug in
the marsh, the mud slipped back in, filling it up again. The
sides had to be propped up immediately.

Then in 1819, canal diggers were bugged by a problem
they could not solve. Even though it was very small, its
consequences were large. Legend has it that in the spring of
that year, as one of the contractors gazed at the swamps they
were about to try to clear, a Cayuga Indian warned, "When
the black moschetto stands so upon the wall"—he hunched
his fingers—"men will shake and burn and die." He was
describing the *Anopheles* mosquito and the disease it carried,
known today as malaria.

At first the workers considered the swarms of
mosquitoes to be pests, not life-threatening dangers.
Some men wore "Montezuma necklaces," smudge-buckets
they hung around their necks. A smudge-bucket was a
pail packed with twigs and damp leaves, with a slow fire
deep in it. Supposedly the rising smoke discouraged
the biting insects, but it also choked the wearers.

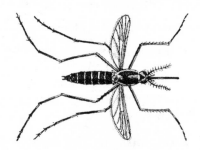

MOSQUITOES ALMOST KILLED THE ERIE CANAL.

They spent as much time coughing as digging.

In August, men began coming down with what they called the "canal shakes" or "ague shakes" (ague is another word for flu). They did not know they had been infected with malaria from the bites of the mosquitoes. Some people claimed that God was making them sick as punishment for building a faster means of travel than nature intended. A thousand men fell ill, and many died. The only treatment at all effective was "Jesuit's bark," a new medicine imported from Peru. Panic struck, and workers who were not too sick to walk fled the "bad air." The digging stopped.

Canal agents scouted for new workers. They promised high wages, good food, free medical care, and "whiskey every night if you get the shakes."

"And a pine box in the morning," listeners replied as they refused the job.

It looked like the grand Erie Canal was sunk forever in the slime and ooze of the Montezuma swamps, a project killed by biting mosquitoes.

On a personal level, DeWitt Clinton and his family knew about the dangers of mosquitoes. The summer before, disease carried by mosquitoes probably contributed to the death of his wife, Maria. The Clintons had been married for 22 years, and they had ten children. She was suffering poor health, but the inescapable swarms of insects seemed to make her condition worse. On July 30, 1818, she died at age 42.

But canal construction came back to life.

Chapter Five

WELL BEGUN, FAR FROM DONE

W HEN THE AUTUMN OF 1819 CAME, ITS chilly weather killed the mosquitoes. People stopped getting sick. James Geddes, determined to take advantage of this positive change, posted an ad in the local newspaper. He said he wanted to buy gloves. Women in the region read his ad and took up their knitting needles. He bought the gloves they made not for himself, but for the sake of the canal. He wanted to keep men's hands warm so that work could be done when it was safe—in the mosquito-free winter. He advertised for workers, and 300 of them stepped forward. Normally no one would even try to dig in the snowy winter, but in Montezuma, digging ground that was half-frozen was easier than digging in summertime mud that oozed back into every hole as soon as it was made.

MANY WORKERS PUT IN LONG HOURS AND BACK-BREAKING LABOR DURING THE CONSTRUCTION OF THE CANAL.

When it wasn't snowing too hard or the temperature was not
unbearably cold, the men made so much progress that the
section was completed by the next spring.

But other problems now arose. How could the canal lock
walls be made to hold water? They were constructed of rocks
and stones, but some kind of cement was needed to make
them watertight. Otherwise, the water would seep out, slowly
emptying the canal and making the land next to it soggy.

At first, construction crews tried using a substance called
quicklime. It was an easy-to-make chemical compound
often used to speed the hardening of mortar, the cement-
like material that fills the gaps between rocks or bricks in a
wall. But quicklime did not work for this job. The constant
exposure to water made it fall apart. If the walls could not
hold water, the canal would indeed be nothing more than
a dry ditch—"Clinton's Folly," as his opponents continued
to call it. Clinton researched the problem and discovered
a cement used in Rome, Italy, that might work well. He
ordered samples, but there was not enough money to import
the quantity they would need to line the entire canal with it.

Canvass White came up with a solution. He was an
assistant of Benjamin Wright, the middle section's head
engineer. White was so devoted to the success of the canal
that he had paid his own way to England to study the
canals there so that he could apply that knowledge to the
building of the Erie. But it was in Chittenango, a village
near Syracuse, New York, that he found the answer to the

problem of the leaking walls. It was a common rock called limestone. When ground up, the limestone could be mixed with sand to create a mortar. To test whether the mixture was truly waterproof, he and Andrew Barto, a scientist, rolled it into a ball, and set it in a pail of water. If it stayed hard and firm overnight, White figured the material might do the trick. It passed the test. White experimented further to get the limestone-sand mixture just right. A factory was set up nearby to manufacture this cement. More than 400,000 bushels of it were used to seal the walls of the entire canal.

IF THE WALLS COULD NOT HOLD WATER, THE CANAL WOULD INDEED BE NOTHING MORE THAN A DRY DITCH—"CLINTON'S FOLLY," AS HIS OPPONENTS CONTINUED TO CALL IT.

By the end of the second year of the canal's construction, impatient citizens wanted to try part of it. But although almost 90 percent of the middle section had been dug, it still wasn't quite ready to be filled with water and put to use. To prove the canal's worth to supporters who were starting to doubt its value, Clinton promised that the first 16-mile stretch between Rome and Utica would be opened in the fall of 1819. His political enemies laughed at the slow progress.

They said that if it took two years to open up only 16 miles, would the 363-mile ditch ever be completed? The project seemed like a money-eating hole. His critics jeered, "Why grin? It will do to bury its mad author in."

When the day came to fill the first section of the canal, emergency crews were stationed at intervals to repair any leaks. Workers opened gates into the canal from feeder streams, and the water started pouring into the ditch. Canvass White patrolled the towpath at a gallop, noting the figures shouted by the men who stood holding yardsticks in the middle of the ditch. "One foot and rising," "foot and a half," "two foot and coming fast." Imitating the town crier, one called "three foot and all's well." Then came the final "four foot," passing in shouts across the miles. When the canal depth rose to four feet, the gates from the feeder streams were closed. At last holding water, the ditch had become an artificial river. Only a few soft spots leaked, and repair crews quickly plugged them.

On October 22, 1819, DeWitt Clinton and the other canal commissioners proudly rode in the first boat to ply the canal's waters. It was named the *Chief Engineer* in honor of Benjamin Wright. Built in Rome, New York, especially for this occasion, it was 61 feet long but weighed very little. Only one horse was needed to pull it from Rome to Utica, a 16-mile trip that took four hours. In a letter to the *Albany Daily Advertiser*, one observer at the occasion wrote that excited spectators "were running across the fields, climbing on trees and fences, and

crowding the bank of the canal to gaze upon the welcome
sight." The enthusiastic crowd saw that the boat's smooth and
easy speed, four miles per hour, was a huge improvement over
traveling in a slow, bumpy wagon. It seemed that the Erie
Canal just might live up to the promises of its promoters—but
construction was far from complete.

A CROWD CHEERS THE OPENING OF THE ERIE CANAL.

THE ERIE CANAL IN SYRACUSE

In 1820 the entire middle section was finished, filled with water, and opened for use. At the Fourth of July celebration in Syracuse, decorated boats carried cheering, waving passengers. Even though only one-fourth of the canal was built, the use of that much of it, plus the construction work on the rest of it, brought great prosperity to the region. In 1820, New York's population had grown so much that it became the nation's largest state. It would stay number one for 150 years.

Boat-building businesses sprang up to make vessels for the canal. The boats had to be low enough to cruise under canal bridges, small enough to fit into locks, and suitable for being pulled by a horse or mule. They were made of wood. Most, called line boats, were designed to carry freight. Boats for passenger travel were called packets, named after the large sailing ships that transported passengers across the Atlantic.

The canal was busy with traffic virtually from the moment it opened. Eager to try the waterway, families living along it built their own boats, many of which were poorly constructed. Professional boaters complained that the homemade vessels sank and became obstacles in their path. Loggers also used the canal, floating timbers tied together in loose rafts.

THE ERIE CANAL IN SCHENECTADY

On the towpath, horses and mules pulling boats competed for space with fishermen, as well as sportsmen engaging in horse and foot races. Couples strolled along, children played games, and vendors lined the towpath

HORSES, RATHER THAN MULES, PULLED THE SPEEDY PACKET
BOATS DESIGNED FOR PASSENGER TRAVEL.

**POISONOUS RATTLESNAKES LIKED TO SUN THEMSELVES
ON THE TOWPATH.**

selling everything from potatoes to pots. To solve the
crowding problem, fines were imposed to keep people who
did not belong there off the towpath. Animals were not so
easily removed. Poisonous rattlesnakes sunned themselves
on the towpath. They posed a constant danger for the
hoggees (the Scottish word for laborers), as the boys who led
the mules were called. Many Irish farmers brought bowls of
Irish soil with them when they immigrated to America, and
legend has it that Irish hoggees were given some of the dirt
to scatter along the path. Because Ireland had no snakes, the
hoggees hoped its soil would rid the towpath of them.

Busy though it was, this stretch was only the canal's
midsection. It was an isolated ribbon of water, not the full
connection between the Hudson River and Lake Erie. Digging
the eastern section from Utica to Albany, and the western part
from Seneca Falls to Lake Erie, would be more expensive and
more difficult than the middle had been. Just how much more
difficult, the canal builders were about to discover.

Chapter Six

ALL THE WAY—ALMOST

T HE MOST CHALLENGING WORK LAY AHEAD. The eastern and western sections of the Erie Canal crossed mountains and rivers. Clinton and the other canal commissioners worried. Would workers be able to build a canal up and over sheer cliffs? Could they build aqueducts strong enough to carry the canal over rivers as wide as the Mohawk and Genesee? Would public opinion, fueled by politicians who disliked the powerful Governor Clinton, turn against this expensive project?

By 1820, after three years of work, barely one-fourth of the canal had opened. About 275 miles had yet to be built. There was no time to lose. Construction continued from both ends of the middle section, heading west toward Buffalo and Lake Erie and east toward Albany and the Hudson River.

THE UPPER FALLS OF THE GENESEE RIVER IN ROCHESTER, NEW YORK. THE ERIE CANAL HAD TO CROSS THE GENESEE RIVER, ONE OF MANY CHALLENGES CANAL BUILDERS FACED IN THE WESTERN PART OF THE STATE.

Because the middle section was flat, it had no locks, but in the eastern and western parts of the canal route, the elevation changed dramatically. Many locks were needed. Early critics of the canal idea had said, "You can't make water go uphill," but thanks to locks, there was a way to carry boats uphill.

A *lock* is a chamber with gates on both ends. One of the gates is always closed. When a canal boat enters a lock, the closed gate is in front of it. After the boat goes inside the lock, the gate behind it also closes. If the next section of the canal is higher, then the boat must be lifted up to that height. To do that, water from upstream is allowed to drain into the lock,

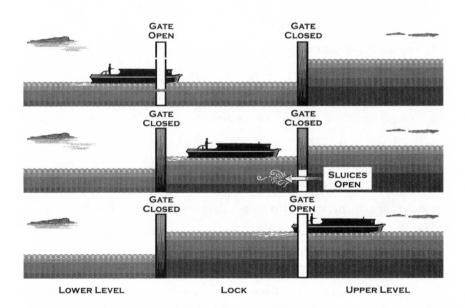

HOW A LOCK WORKS

increasing the depth of the water in the lock and raising the boat floating on it. Or, if the next section is lower, then water in the lock is released. When the water in the lock reaches the same height as the water on the next stretch of the canal, the gate in front of the boat is opened, and the boat comes out of the lock. This way, a lock safely carries boats to a different elevation, whether they need to be raised or lowered. As a result, boats do not need to deal with rapids or waterfalls that a natural river might tumble over.

BOATS WAITING THEIR TURN TO ENTER A LOCK

Canvass White had visited canals in England and studied their locks. His information helped the Erie planners design 83 locks, each 90 feet long, 15 feet wide, and eight feet four inches high. Constructing them would take money, skill, and time. Money was tight, and each lock cost more than $8,000, a huge sum in those days. Skill was gained only through experience. As for the time, when Clinton's political enemies complained about the slow pace of construction, he promised the canal would be completed by 1823. A huge amount of work still remained to be done. The best way to speed the canal's progress would be to add more workers.

Local residents proved invaluable in canal construction, but there were not that many of them. In 1820 the population of the entire western part of the state was just over 100,000 people, with fewer than eight people per square mile. Some farmers were hired as contractors to oversee work crews near their land, but many of them did not have much time for canal work. Some freed slaves also worked on the canal. One engineer used convict labor, but this was not typical. Where could enough workers be found who would be willing to dig their way through the wilderness, day after day, in the heat, the rain, or the cold?

Desperate for jobs, many new immigrants answered the call. Recent arrivals from England, Scotland, Wales, and Germany helped build the canal, but the most famous of the workers were the Irish. Large numbers of single Irish men were arriving in New York City. As soon as they got off their boats, representatives from the canal approached them at the pier in New York City.

When told about the job, the immigrants asked, "What's the pay?"

"Fifty cents and found," answered the canal people. "Found" meant food and lodging.

IRISH IMMIGRANTS ARRIVING IN NEW YORK CITY SUPPLIED SOME OF THE LABOR THAT BUILT THE ERIE CANAL.

"A week?" asked the Irish, accustomed to making 80 cents a week in Ireland.

"No, a day!" was the answer. Irish workers flocked to the job.

Because so much of the canal was dug in remote areas, camps were set up where the men ate and slept. They worked Monday through Saturday. Their 14-hour days began a half-hour before sunrise with the cook yelling, "All out! Mush on the kettle." But they ate more than mush (cornmeal boiled in water). Breakfast might also include bacon, eggs, sausage, pork chops, ham, potatoes, corn bread, rolls, or pancakes with molasses and syrup. To have the strength and stamina to do the job, the men needed plenty of fuel.

Food was usually purchased from local trappers and farmers. If the crew was working far away from a town, sometimes a contractor might bring a cow along to provide milk. At night, wild game such as venison, bear, or partridge was often served. If the canal work was progressing well, there might be a Saturday night feast to celebrate. The main feature of it would be a huge stew. Some cooks made pumpkin pies that measured two feet across. Whiskey flowed freely. Music played on a harmonica or Jew's harp cheered the party, and sometimes people sang traditional songs as well as ones they made up about their canal.

In spite of the plentiful food, workers found the living conditions hard. The beds were usually nothing more than boards lined up inside a rough shack that slept 30 or 40 men. It was said that "hickory lasts longer, but pine sleeps softer." No matter how uncomfortable the boards, the exhausted men usually managed to sleep. But some of the Irish were kept up at night because of the hooting owls and screeching wildcats. The immigrants were fearful of the unfamiliar animals in the American wilderness. The first time a snake came into camp, some of the Irish nearly

WHERE COULD ENOUGH WORKERS BE FOUND WHO WOULD BE WILLING TO DIG THEIR WAY THROUGH THE WILDERNESS, DAY AFTER DAY, IN THE HEAT, THE RAIN, OR THE COLD?

deserted. There are no snakes in Ireland, and they thought this one was the devil.

By 1821, about 9,000 men were working on the eastern and western sections of the canal. Although the Irish immigrants probably made up only about one-fourth to one-third of the canal workforce, their fun-loving, hard-working presence made them the most famous. They boasted that they clawed out the canal with their bare fingers and then filled it with their honest sweat. They were proud of their "canawl," as they called it. They said, "God made the rivers, but the Irish made the canal."

When workers tackled the eastern section beyond Utica, they faced a challenge right away. In the course of only eight miles, the land's elevation dropped more than one hundred feet. Thirteen locks needed to be built almost one right after another in order to lower the boats traveling from west to east, or to raise them if they were traveling in the other direction. Using plans based on Canvass White's information about English canal locks, the crews dug the canal and built the locks. By the end of 1821, 24 miles of the canal were opened in the eastern section between Utica and Little Falls, and work was progressing on the final rugged stretch through the Mohawk River Valley from Little Falls all the way to Albany.

In the western end of the state, another kind of challenge was tackled, one that locks could not handle. The problem was how to deal with flowing water—rivers! The canal could not intersect a natural waterway without being swept apart by the current. Therefore the canal was carried over creeks and rivers on water bridges called aqueducts. Eighteen were built, the largest one over the Genesee River in Rochester. It took two years to build this aqueduct, which was both graceful and very strong. Supported by 11 Roman-style arches, it held up 2,000 tons (four million pounds) of canal water.

Another challenge east of Rochester called for yet another kind of solution. The canal needed to cross Irondequoit (i-RON-da-koit) Creek. Although called a creek, it was really the size of a river. It ran through a 70-foot-deep valley whose sides were one mile apart. An aqueduct crossing it would

**IT TOOK TWO YEARS TO BUILD THE AQUEDUCT
THAT CARRIED THE ERIE CANAL OVER THE GENESEE RIVER IN
ROCHESTER, NEW YORK.**

have to be a mile long, so that was not a practical possibility.
Engineers decided instead to direct Irondequoit Creek
through a tunnel under the canal. They had workers make
a gigantic wall of dirt, a mound 70 feet high and 245 feet
wide. This "embankment," as they called it, stretched all the
way across the valley, and the canal was built along its top. To
avoid causing a flood as a result of blocking the flow of the
creek, they installed a stone culvert, like a huge pipe, at the
bottom of the embankment for the creek to flow through.

Progress was being made, but the canal still had a long
way to go.

Chapter Seven

LOCKING UP AND DOWN

ITH GROWING EXPERIENCE, CANAL builders were gaining knowledge about the construction of locks, but one site posed a problem far greater than any dealt with so far. It was a rock cliff 66 feet high. Only 17 miles away, the same rock formation caused the Niagara River to drop in a spectacular cascade known as Niagara Falls. One of the canal commissioners, William Bouck, was in charge of this section. He invited engineers to submit plans for how the canal could get over this rock wall. Nathan Roberts, a school principal, created the winning design. It came to be known as the "Lockport Combine," a series of five pairs of locks in a row. Like stair steps, they would allow boats to climb the cliff, or escarpment. Each lock would have a lift of 12 feet instead of the usual eight feet

THE LOCKPORT COMBINE SOLVED ONE OF THE BIGGEST PROBLEMS
IN THE CONSTRUCTION OF THE ERIE —
HOW TO RAISE AND LOWER BOATS OVER A 66-FOOT-HIGH CLIFF.

four inches. These locks would be built side by side so traffic could move in both directions, similar to up and down escalators. Otherwise, the bottleneck of boats waiting to pass through the five locks would back up traffic for miles.

Before work on this section of the canal began, the site of the future Lockport Combine was nothing more than a clearing in the forest at the edge of the cliff. Only three families lived there. In less than six months after construction began, 337 families called it home.

Nathan Roberts had developed an excellent design, but how could it be turned into reality? How could canal builders dig a ditch through three miles of solid rock consisting of hard dolomite limestone and even harder flint? The strongest workers with spades and pickaxes could not do it The engineers decided to try blasting it out of the way using an explosive manufactured by French immigrant E.I. du Pont. For about 20 years, his Delaware company had been making a new formula of gunpowder called "black powder." It was reputed to be more reliable than the primitive explosives available previously. (Dynamite would not be invented for another half-century.) Miners came to show the canal builders how to use the explosive.

To begin making what they called the Deep Cut in the cliff, workers first needed to drill holes to put the blasting powder into. They used handheld drills, for there were no power drills then. The drill bits often broke. Once they succeeded in cutting a deep enough hole, they filled it with the du Pont powder almost to the brim and pressed it down with clay. Sometimes they asked a young boy to light the fuse that would cause the powder to explode. It was thought that the youth could run more quickly than an adult could to get away from the dangerous blast.

IT SOUNDED LIKE INDEPENDENCE DAY, MUSTER DAY, AND THE THUNDERS OF DOOMSDAY, ALL IN ONE.

There were very few controls over the size of each explosion. Huge chunks of rock often flew in unexpected directions. Townspeople put up tree trunk walls in front of their houses for protection. The constant blasts made the earth shake. One resident said it "sounded like Independence Day, Muster Day, and the thunders of Doomsday, all in one." Inexperience with the powerful explosive made accidents common, and some workers lost their lives.

Once the rock was blasted loose, something had to be done with the piles of rubble left behind. To clear it out of the way, engineers designed cranes that lowered huge buckets down to the heap of rocks strewn every which way after each blast. Men lifted the rocks into the buckets, and horses pulled cables that swung the buckets up and away from the cut. These cranes lined the route as the cut was made.

Digging the Deep Cut and building the locks would take two and a half years to complete.

Although canal construction was progressing in spite of the engineering challenges, the man most responsible for getting the project started, DeWitt Clinton, was not faring well. Canal supporters praised his achievements, but his political enemies did not like him as a person, and they especially did not like his power. The majority of the New York State legislature belonged to the political party opposed to Clinton. They appointed the canal commissioners, so

AFTER THE ROCK WAS BLASTED,
CRANES POWERED BY MEN AND HORSES LIFTED IT OUT OF THE
DEEP CUT IN LOCKPORT, NEW YORK.

when positions on the five-member commission opened up, they chose replacements who were anti-Clinton. Those against the governor gained the majority on the commission, and as a result, Clinton lost his control over it.

Political name-calling and lack of cooperation with lawmakers plagued Clinton's every move. Politicians against him who had originally been against the canal insisted they had actually been for it. They claimed Clinton worked for the canal only for his own personal political gain, not because he really believed in it. He was barely reelected governor in 1820. His rash promise that the canal would be completed by 1823 was clearly not going to be kept.

THE COMPLETED DEEP CUT IN LOCKPORT, NEW YORK

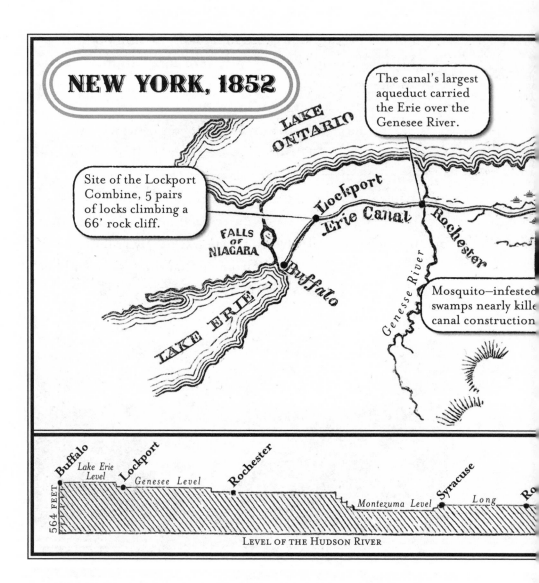

NEW YORK, 1852

The canal's largest aqueduct carried the Erie over the Genesee River.

Site of the Lockport Combine, 5 pairs of locks climbing a 66' rock cliff.

LAKE ONTARIO

Lockport

Erie Canal

Rochester

FALLS OF NIAGARA

Buffalo

Genesse River

Mosquito—infested swamps nearly kille canal construction

LAKE ERIE

Buffalo
Lake Erie Level
Lockport
Genesee Level
Rochester
Montezuma Level
Syracuse
Long
Ro

564 FEET

LEVEL OF THE HUDSON RIVER

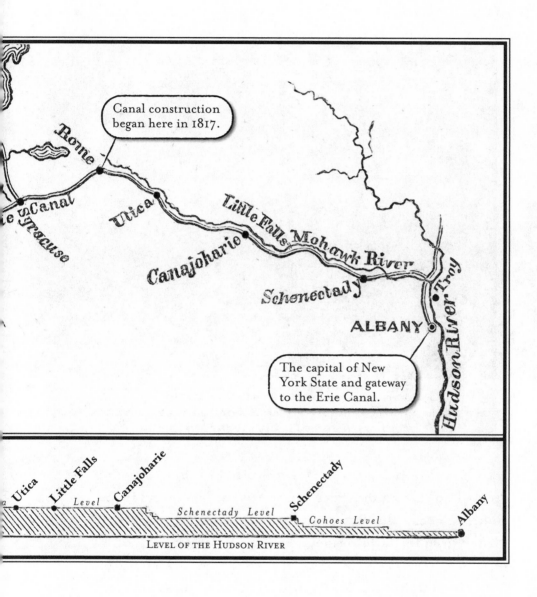

Canal construction began here in 1817.

The capital of New York State and gateway to the Erie Canal.

WITH 83 LOCKS, THE ERIE CANAL CLIMBED AND DROPPED 675 FEET AS IT CROSSED NEW YORK STATE.

BUILDING THE LOCKPORT COMBINE — TWO SETS OF
FIVE LOCKS IN A ROW — DEMANDED NEW TECHNOLOGY, AND ITS CONSTRUCTION
TOOK MORE THAN TWO YEARS TO COMPLETE.

When Clinton's two-year term expired in 1822, he decided not to run for office again. Instead, he would focus on his beloved canal as a commissioner. Clinton received a letter from former President Thomas Jefferson, now 80 years old. Jefferson wrote that New York State was a hundred years ahead of its time for its success in building a canal, a technological achievement that Jefferson had not believed possible. Clinton must have felt a great deal of pride.

Then, in spite of the advances of the canal, Clinton's political career seemed in danger of slipping even further back. In the spring of 1824, the legislature, controlled by anti-Clinton men, removed Clinton from the canal commission. But their move backfired. Instead of losing power, he gained the sympathy of the people of New York. They were outraged by the injustice of his being yanked from the commission. Thousands held protest rallies in Albany and New York City, where no building was large enough to accommodate the crowd. The People's Party nominated Clinton to run for governor in the upcoming election. He won.

By the time General Lafayette, the French hero of the American Revolution, made a return visit to America, he was able to tour an almost-completed canal in June 1825. He rode on a boat named *Governor Clinton*.

Excitement ran high all summer long as the final section of the canal was dug from the Lockport Combine to Lake Erie. Local people cheered on the crew, offering free whiskey and applause to the fastest workers.

When the opening ceremonies were held in Buffalo that October day in 1825, the people of New York State and their wildly popular governor, DeWitt Clinton, had reason to be proud. Overcoming huge natural, financial, and political hurdles, they had built Clinton's Ditch, the grand Erie Canal.

Could it live up to its promise?

Chapter Eight

LOW BRIDGE

URING THE COLD AND SNOWY WINTERS, the canal was closed for boating because the water would freeze over. To prevent ice from damaging the walls, and to make maintenance easier, most of the water was drained out. But the winter of 1825-1826 proved to be relatively mild. After only a few freezing months, the canal was reopened in late February. Opponents of canal construction had said nobody would use it. They were wrong. Boats crowded the canal right away. In the canal's first full season, $750,000 was collected in tolls. That money—even more than Governor Clinton had hoped for the first year—helped pay for the construction costs.

The tolls were usually based on how much a boat weighed. A hydraulic weigh lock with metal scales at the waterline measured the weight of a boat when empty, and

PASSENGERS OCCASIONALLY WALKED THE TOWPATH AND JUMPED BACK ON THEIR PACKET BOAT FROM A LOW BRIDGE.

then when it was loaded with cargo. At first, a few boat
owners tried to avoid paying the fees. At night, they would
sneak past the toll collectors in the darkness. They wrapped
rags around their horses' feet to muffle their sound.
Outsmarting them, the toll collector at Rome made a chain
fence that he lowered into the canal at dusk. He "netted"
boats trying to sneak past.

Many different kinds of boats traveled on the canal.
The grandest were the packets, noted for passengers' deluxe
accommodations and the speed at which the boat traveled.
One passenger from Rochester wrote that she hoped God
was not offended by the high speed that seemed to her like
"flying." Packets had the right of way. Slower boats had to
allow them to pass, and packets had first priority at the locks.

Packet captains knew they were the kings of the canal,
and many looked the part. A captain might wear a tall beaver
hat, a fine brass-buttoned coat, a flashy neckcloth fastened
with a cameo or even a diamond stickpin, bright trousers,
and imported leather boots. Such a well-dressed man was
nicknamed a "macaroni" or "dandy," terms many kids know
today from the traditional song "Yankee Doodle Dandy."
The captain made an elegant picture as he stood proudly on
the deck tooting loud, clear notes on his horn. Asserting his
right of way, the macaroni puffed up his chest and pulled
first into the lock as the other boats waited their turn.

In the 1840s, about 40 packet boats cruised the canal.
They each used three horses, exchanging them for fresh

ones every 12 or 15 miles. Many other boats did not travel on Sunday, but packet boats often ran day and night, seven days a week. Four miles per hour was the legal limit, but often the speediest packets hit six or even seven miles per hour, openly disobeying the limit. The captain would readily pay the ten-dollar fine, for his profits rose far more than that when he traveled quickly and could take on new passengers. Packets ran regularly between Albany and Buffalo in four to six days.

A BOAT LEAVES A LOCK AND CONTINUES ON ITS WAY
UNDER THE LIGHT OF A FULL MOON.

A large packet boat might carry up to one hundred people. Agents hired by the packets competed for passengers, saying their boat had the best food, most comfortable beds, and fastest horses. One advertised with this verse, suggesting that passengers could expect high-quality service because the packet's stewards hoped to win a promotion to captain:

> Our Boats are fine, them none surpass,
> Our captains polite, if only ask'd
> And Stewards wide awake, you'll see-
> For captains-they expect to be.

**PASSENGERS SOCIALIZED AND ENJOYED THE PASSING VIEW FROM
THE ROOF OF THEIR ELEGANT PACKET BOAT.**

In good weather, passengers sat on the roof, chatted
with other travelers, enjoyed the scenery, and played guitars
and flutes. During bad weather, they might retreat to the
cabin, often carpeted and hung with curtains, where they
could read selections from the boat's library of books and
newspapers. Passengers typically paid four to five cents per
mile, with the fare including three hearty meals a day.

At bedtime, narrow canvas bunks were put up along the
walls of the packets. Men remained on deck until the women

and children had gone to bed in the front of the cabin. Then the men descended to their own bunks curtained off from the other sleeping quarters. Stacked two or three high, with little space between them, sleepers sometimes complained that they could not turn over. British author Charles Dickens made a trip on a packet boat and compared sleepers on the narrow tiers of bunks to books wedged into library shelves. One traveler said that he awoke breathless because of a heavy weight on his chest. He managed to free his hand to poke a stickpin into the canvas that pressed him down. He awoke the snoring sleeper above him, whose bulk had caused the canvas to tear, allowing its heavy occupant to droop onto the sleeper below. When George M. Pullman traveled on a packet, he was so impressed by the sleeping system that he used it as a model in the railroad sleeping cars he invented.

Packet boats were painted brightly, with their names and home ports written across the stern. They had grand names like the *Starry Flag*, *American Spy*, *Try to Catch Me*, *Poor Richard*, *Rip Van Winkle*, *Humility*, *Merry Fiddler*, and *Fair Play*. Some names showed a sense of humor. Because the canal was level and shallow, the boats never had to navigate rough open seas. But some of the canal boats' names suggested otherwise: *Queen of the Waves*, *Stormy Lass*, *Sea Rover*, and *Pirate's Pride*. Similarly, popular songs contained humorous lyrics about the "dangers" of the Erie. Composer Stephen Foster mentioned the "raging canal" in his "Song of All Songs," and author Mark Twain wrote a poem about "The Aged Pilot Man" who saved a ship on a stormy Erie Canal.

Travelers on all the boats, even the splendid packets, quickly learned to take the warning "Low bridge" seriously.

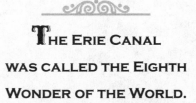

THE ERIE CANAL

WAS CALLED THE EIGHTH

WONDER OF THE WORLD.

Farmers whose land was crossed by the canal had been promised that "occupation bridges" would be built so they could continue their occupation of farming even if the canal split their land. To save money, the bridges were made as small and low as possible. About 300 of them were built, only seven and a half feet above water. People who failed to duck, or sometimes even lie flat on the roof of a boat, could be scraped off by the bridge and dumped into the canal. Of course, the canal was only four feet deep, so there was little danger of drowning. But dignified gentlemen and ladies did not want a rude dumping in the Ditch! Author Nathaniel Hawthorne wrote that one schoolteacher seated on the packet's roof was so busy reading a book that when the helmsman yelled, "Bridge!" the teacher did not duck. Instead, Hawthorne said, "he was saluted by said bridge on

NIAGARA FALLS

his knowledge-box." Fortunately he was not hurt seriously, ending up with only a large bump on his head and perhaps a dent in his ego, too. Some passengers chose to stretch their legs, getting off the boat at a lock and walking alongside until they could jump back on from a low bridge.

Tourists of all kinds came to cruise on the famous canal, view the engineering marvel of the Lockport Combine, cross aqueducts over mighty rivers, and experience the world's safest, fastest form of transportation. Suffragist Susan B.

Anthony traveled west to Rochester on the Erie. Tycoon Leland B. Stanford, founder of the world-renowned university in California, also traveled on the Erie. Nathaniel Hawthorne wrote his overall impression of traveling the canal: "In my imagination Dewitt Clinton was an enchanter, who had waved his magic wand from the Hudson to Lake Erie."

The Erie Canal was called the Eighth Wonder of the World, and it provided access to one of the original Seven Wonders of the World—Niagara Falls. Thanks to the canal, the tourist industry boomed at Niagara Falls, only a few miles from the canal. Niagara Falls State Park became—and to this day continues to be—one of the most visited parks in the United States.

Chapter Nine

ON THE MOVE

PACKET BOATS CARRIED PASSENGERS AND their hand luggage, but they had no room for the gear and supplies accompanying immigrant families moving west. These travelers usually booked cheaper passage on line boats, which transported freight and livestock. Line boats allowed travelers to set up camp and cookstoves on deck. Sometimes whole families slept in the open air on top of their belongings.

Far more numerous than the packets, line boats were much slower, usually pulled by one pair of mules or horses. These animals were brought on board and kept in stalls when they were not working. Packets commonly covered 80 miles in a 24-hour period, and often more. In contrast, line boats generally ran only during daylight and made at most about 60 miles in a day, and often less. But even travel on

ERIE CANAL BOATS DOCKED IN BUFFALO

the line boats was still much faster, cheaper, and safer than an overland trip.

In the first year after the canal opened, 40,000 settlers used it to go west. Immigrants from Ireland, England, Germany, Norway, and Holland crowded the line boats' decks. Many New England farmers joined the migration, too. Disgusted with their poor, rocky soil, they were lured west by stories about inexpensive land that raised a hundred bushels of corn to an acre and hogs that grew fat just rooting on acorns and beechnuts. The forests near the canal provided game at no cost, so even the poorest families could eat well on the trip. Below the decks, the line boats carried tools, clocks, guns, needles, cloth, and other manufactured items for the settlers.

After crossing New York on the canal, travelers boarded steamboats in Buffalo and set out onto Lake Erie. By 1831, as many as a thousand immigrants a day passed through Buffalo bound for Ohio and beyond. Buffalo itself was transformed from a village to a bustling city. The *Buffalo Journal* said in 1830 that "our children are surrounded by the comforts, the blessings and the elegances of life, where their fathers found only hardship, privation and want."

Some immigrants stopped before reaching Buffalo. They established new communities along the canal. It was not uncommon for a family who owned their own boat to take it apart when they reached the spot where they wanted to settle. They recycled the best wood from their boat, using it

**THE UNDERGROUND RAILROAD HELPED
SLAVES ESCAPE TO FREEDOM IN CANADA. SOME OF THEM TRAVELED
NOT ONLY ON LAND, BUT ALSO ON THE ERIE CANAL.**

to build their new home on land. If their boat started to fall
apart before the family got to the place they had planned to
settle, they might just change their plans and put down roots
wherever their boat gave out.

A few users of the canal planned not to settle down,
but to escape. The Erie Canal served in the Underground
Railroad, the network of people who helped slaves flee to

freedom. After traveling on the canal to Buffalo, escaping slaves made their way to nearby Canada.

The canal stayed busy. It was common for as many as 250 boats to pass through a lock each day. By 1850 there were so many traffic jams at locks that boats lined up, bow to stern, for miles waiting their turn. Fights broke out between crewmembers competing to have their boat enter a lock first. Unpopular with all the other boats were timber rafts. Long and clumsy, they were pulled by oxen at only a mile and a half an hour. Sometimes these rafts were several hundred feet long, made of as many as ten sections of logs, called "cribs," hitched together. The cribs had to be separated at locks so they could pass through one at a time. While this was going on, all the line boats had to wait.

Just as fast-food restaurants, gas stations, and convenience stores today are clustered at freeway interchanges, stores sprang up at canal locks 150 years ago. They sold almost anything a boat or its passengers might need. Kids loved to snack while they helped their mothers shop. Many storekeepers left an open barrel of pickles and crackers and a huge hunk of cheese for people to help themselves to. The same store might have a wide range of goods, including hay, oats, and harnesses for the mules; dishes, pans, and kettles for cooking; washboards for laundry; and all sorts of food.

But the Erie Canal's main purpose was to provide safe, speedy transportation—not convenient shopping. It was clear almost from the moment the canal was opened that it was

GROCERY STORES ALONG THE CANAL PROVIDED TRAVELERS WITH FOOD AND SUPPLIES.

overcrowded and needed to be enlarged. In fact, only ten years after the Wedding of the Waters, the enlarging process began. By 1862 the entire Erie had been widened from 40 to 70 feet, and its depth increased from four to seven feet. Leaky aqueducts were replaced by stronger ones, and single locks were replaced by double ones, allowing boats to pass in

both directions at the same time. Early canal boats carried
30 tons of freight. Bigger boats on the larger canal could
carry as much as 240 tons.

Shipping goods became so much cheaper that huge
markets opened up. Some businessmen in New York City had

THE NEW YORK CITY HARBOR BECAME VERY BUSY AFTER
THE OPENING OF THE ERIE CANAL.

once opposed construction of the canal because they feared
traffic would simply cruise through, taking its wealth with
it. Instead, within 15 years of the canal's opening, New York
City rose from fourth to first place among the nation's ports.
It handled more freight than did New Orleans, Baltimore,
and Boston combined. On the canal, wheat, flour, barley,
potatoes, apples, cider, whiskey, butter, cheese, fowl, lumber,
and furs from the American West were transported to New
York City and from there, shipped to Europe. New York's
harbor served as America's gateway to the world.

DeWitt Clinton's promises of prosperity came true,
but he lived to see only part of their fulfillment. In 1828,
while he was still governor, he died suddenly in his home
in Albany, probably from a heart attack. But his Ditch kept
his memory alive. For a century, it helped enrich almost
everyone who had any connection with it.

Besides making money, the canal also made a new way of life
for thousands of people—not only for pioneers who headed west
but also for families who worked and lived on it.

Chapter Ten

WORKING LIKE A MULE

THE CANAL THAT CUT THROUGH WESTERN New York transformed the landscape it crossed from a wilderness with a few scattered farms and villages to a ribbon of businesses and people from all over the world. Opportunity beckoned, and workers thronged to the region to take advantage of it.

Villages far from a natural waterway were named ports on the canal: Port Byron, Port Gibson, Brockport, Spencerport, Fairport, Weedsport, and Middleport. Many newcomers found jobs relating directly to the canal, such as in boat-building businesses, inns, taverns, blacksmith shops, and livery stables. Farming also flourished, for grains grown in fertile western New York could be quickly shipped to markets in the East. By 1838, Rochester called itself the

BUSINESSES FLOURISHED ALONG THE ERIE CANAL.

"Flour City," the flour-milling capital of the world.

The canal also produced energy that helped generate jobs. Rainwater needed to be steadily released so the canal would not overflow. Gates were opened so it could be sent out in sluices, man-made channels designed for this purpose. The exiting water created a strong current. Its energy was harnessed to power waterwheels for lumber mills or gristmills.

Some people worked on the canal itself, for it needed constant maintenance. Even the slightest leak could drain it, stranding all the boats in the mud at the bottom and flooding the land next to the canal. Pathmasters patrolled their ten-mile sections of the towpath to watch for any breaks in the wall. They carried a bag of manure and hay. If they found a small leak, they stuffed the mixture inside it and stamped it down. A lot of damage could be done by a little animal—the muskrat. Muskrats are rodents that look like small beavers. Using their sharp front claws, they made homes by burrowing into the banks of the canal. Their tunnels weakened the banks until they collapsed. Storms could also cause big leaks. If the pathmaster could not fix the damage by himself, he ran to get help. Any hour of the night or day, the repair crew raced to the site at speeds up to ten miles per hour in their slim "hurry-up boats" pulled by fast horses. These boats were always stocked with emergency supplies such as lanterns, planks, ropes, shovels, axes, and hammers.

When the repair crew could not stop the leak on their own, the pathmaster hurried to nearby houses, taverns, and

**A LITTLE MUSKRAT WHO MADE ITS HOME
IN THE WALLS OF THE CANAL COULD WEAKEN THEM SO MUCH THAT
THEY WOULD GIVE WAY, CAUSING THE CANAL TO DRAIN.**

shops to offer good pay to anyone who could help right away. Sometimes whole families, awakened during a storm by the loud knocking of the pathmaster on their door, stayed up all night to help cut trees or drive a team of oxen. They would haul huge timbers to the canal to dam the leak.

If a break allowed canal water to flood planted fields, farmers could sue the state for the lost crops. Probably the most unusual claim the state paid was not for crops, however, but for an outhouse, or privy, near Bushnell's Basin east of Rochester. The man who owned the outhouse sold tools and

equipment on credit to farmers. He kept no written records
of the transactions other than scratching them into the
privy's wood wall. When the privy washed away due to a break
in the canal, the man said he could not prove who owed him
money. The state gave him the $2,000 he claimed he could
never collect without his privy-wall accounting.

Even with claims such as this, the state of New York

A STEERSMAN GUIDED THE BOAT USING A LONG WOODEN TILLER.

quickly profited from tolls collected on the canal. In just 11 years after the canal opened, it earned enough to pay back all its construction costs.

Much of the canal employment took place on the water. Usually a captain and his family lived day and night on his boat. Some captains owned their boats, while others were hired by the owners for the excellent wage of $50 a month. The captain's wife cooked, washed, and kept house in a tiny cabin. When the boats passed farmland, sometimes "shopping" meant catching corn or potatoes a farmer tossed to the canallers floating by. If a child had a good throw, she might pay the farmer by putting a coin in one potato and tossing it back to him.

Large boats had a crew of five or six: a captain, a cook, two hoggees, and two steersmen. The steersmen shared their job in alternating shifts. They steered the boat with the large rudder moved with a long, heavy tiller. The job was important, for a collision could easily damage the wooden boats. Not only did the steersmen have to watch out for other boats, but they also had to beware of hazards like floating logs, bridge supports, and sunken boats. Typical line boats were 77 feet long and 14 feet 3 inches wide. They just barely fit in the 15-foot-wide locks. A steersman's wages averaged $20 a month plus room and board. Sometimes at night the steersmen sang to pass the time away. Sleepers heard strains of "My Bonnie Lies Over the Ocean," "Paddy on the Canal," or "I Was a Boatsman's Boy."

Speedy packet boats were often pulled by good-looking horses, but slow and steady mules were the most common animals on the towpath. There were so many of them they were nicknamed "long-eared robins." It was said a mule ate a third less than a horse of the same size, but was a third stronger. With their smaller feet, mules had more agility for climbing out of the canal if they fell in. They were generally hardier than horses, too. And those long ears? Some people claimed to forecast the weather by looking at the droop of the mules' ears.

Hoggees were responsible for the mules. In 1845, about 5,000 hoggees worked the towpath. Most of them were between 10 and 15 years old. Usually mules were hitched in

MULES POWERED MOST OF THE BOATS ON THE CANAL.

a team of two or sometimes three, one ahead of the other. Sometimes a hoggee rode the last one, but more often he led them. To pass the time, hoggees might sing:

> Then kick, bite, snort, buck.
> Forget it I never shall,
> The time I drove the sorrel mule
> On the E-rye-ee Canal.

Some hoggees chanted verses like this:

> Hoggee on the towpath five cents a day,
> picking up mule balls to eat along the way,
> Hoggee on the towpath don't know what to say
> walk behind a mule's behind, all the live-long day.

Because there was only one towpath, one boat could pass another only by having the boat on the far side of the canal stop. Its towline would sink, and the passing boat would float over it. If the hoggees weren't careful, however, the towlines might tangle, dragging the mules into the canal.

A hoggee's shift usually lasted six hours, regardless of the weather. After the shift ended, the hoggee led the animals across a ramp on to the boat. He checked to be sure the work collar had not hurt the mules' shoulders, rubbed the animals down with liniment, treated any sores, and repaired the harness. Fresh mules would be led out to take the place

BECAUSE MULES WALKED BOTH DIRECTIONS ON THE ONLY TOWPATH,
WHEN BOATS PASSED EACH OTHER, ONE HAD TO LOWER ITS TOWLINE TO LET THE
OTHER BOAT CROSS OVER IT. THE EASTBOUND BOATS HAD THE RIGHT OF WAY.

of the resting animals. If a family lived on the boat, one son
might handle the first six-hour shift, another the second.
On boats that traveled day and night, each hoggee had two
six-hour shifts. Like the mules, the boys ate and rested
between shifts.

Families with no sons might hire a hoggee, very often
an orphan only 10 or 11 years old. He would live on the
boat with them. If the boy was lucky, he might be treated
like one of the family. But many were not. Some cruel
captains bullied the youngsters. In the early years of

the canal, hoggees earned only ten dollars for the whole season. By the later 1800s, they earned about ten dollars a month. They usually collected their wages only once, at the end of the season when the canal closed during the freezing winter. Some captains purposely mistreated young hoggees in the fall to try to make them run away before they were paid.

In the 1830s about one-fourth of the workers on the canal were children. Besides the boys who took care of the mules, others cleaned the boats. Both boys and girls often helped pump the bilge, ridding the boat of the water that collected onboard. They pumped it back into the canal. In the early spring, children might help caulk and paint a boat

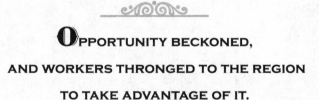

OPPORTUNITY BECKONED,

AND WORKERS THRONGED TO THE REGION

TO TAKE ADVANTAGE OF IT.

to make it ready for the season. Throughout the year, most girls sewed and helped with the cooking, just as they would be expected to do if they lived on land.

It was not unusual for men who worked on the canal to use their earnings on Saturday nights to drink and gamble at canal-side taverns. They got a bad reputation for drinking

too much, fighting, and getting in trouble with the law.
Some canallers carried grudges against the crews of
other boats if they had argued about who could pass or
enter a lock first.

If two packets came upon each other, each going the
opposite direction, the canal rule was that eastbound boats
had the right of way. The westbound boat had to stop and
let its tow ropes go slack in the water, so the eastbound
boat could cruise over them. But if both boats were going
the same direction and one wanted to pass the other, the

THE ERIE CANAL WAS A CENTER OF ACTIVITY.

men in the slower boat sometimes refused to stop and let the other boat pass. Towpath fights were common. In the worst disputes, a crewmember might even cut the tow ropes of another boat. More than once, towpath fights were continued at the bar on Saturday night.

Conservative townspeople warned their children to keep away from the rough canallers. Herman Melville, an author who traveled on the Erie, wrote in his novel *Moby-Dick* that a canaller injected "terror to the smiling innocence of the villages through which he floats." In the mid-19th century, one-fourth of the convicts at the prison in Auburn, New York, had worked on the canal. Some claimed they had gotten drunk and arrested on purpose in the fall so as to have a free place to stay until the canal reopened in the spring.

Many religious folks disapproved of the canallers who worked on Sundays. They considered Sunday a Christian holy day for resting and attending church. In 1825, 12 counties and 18 towns petitioned to ban the use of the canal on Sundays. However, no ban was enacted. It was probably easier to look the other way when it came to canallers working seven days a week, for that seemed better than the alternative—the presence of the idle men on shore, hanging around with nothing constructive to do every Sunday.

Many families who lived on the canal resented the bad image of the rowdy workers. They tried to live as much like their counterparts on land as they could. For them, the canal was not just a place to work. It was a place called home.

Chapter Eleven

AT HOME ON A CANAL BOAT

ALTHOUGH THE CABINS THAT CANAL BOAT families lived in were small, they often had carpets, curtains, and framed pictures on the walls. Kids might have a toy box that held a doll, a set of marbles, tops, and whistles. Instead of playing house, the kids played boat. On a rainy day, a feather from a seagull could provide free entertainment, with kids blowing to keep it aloft. On sunny days, children might make a tent on deck, crawl inside, and create their own games with toy mules. As their boat approached a lock, kids might get to blow the horn to alert the lockkeeper.

Women watched over their youngest children carefully. To protect toddlers, a mother might chain them to the boat! If a child slid off the deck into the canal, the rattling chain would call her to the rescue.

PARENTS RAISED CHILDREN IN THEIR CANAL BOAT HOMES.

Some poor families lived on a "shanty boat." This was a flat boat with a small shack built on it. They might tie up for months at a time at a wide spot in the canal.

There was no indoor plumbing on canal boats. Toilet pots were emptied directly into the canal. But the canal was big enough that even with this pollution, fish were plentiful. Many kids loved to fish and to take a swim on hot summer afternoons.

Sometimes children teased each other with word games and riddles like this one:

> Two brothers we are,
> Great burdens we bear,
> By which we are bitterly pressed.
> In truth we may say,
> We are full all the day,
> But empty when we go to rest.

The answer? Shoes!

The scenery always changed as the boats traveled along. Many floating businesses sold their wares to boaters as well as people along the shore. For example, shops of tinkers, sellers of potions and liniments, and hundreds of other enterprises traveled from village to village. What excitement when kids spied a floating ice cream vendor or the library boat!

**CHILDREN WHO LIVED ON CANAL BOATS ENJOYED PLAYING WITH
DOLLS, TOPS, AND TOY BOATS.**

Sometimes a "bum boat" might row up alongside. It
was called a bum boat because it was not pulled by mules
or horses. Instead, it was tied to other boats, "bumming" a
ride. A family could buy goods—including fresh food—from
a bum boat without having to stop their own boat. After the
sale, the bum boat would untie and hitch a ride with the
next boat that came along.

Families usually traveled from April through November.
Parents who knew how to read did the schooling, teaching
their children from magazines or books like McGuffey's
Readers and the Bible. One of the favorites was *Marco Paul's
Travels on the Erie Canal,* a fictional story published in 1852.

In the winter, boats could not travel the canal because it
was partially drained. Some stayed in basins, wide sections
of the canal that had room for many boats to tie up. Where
the canal was dry, kids might search the empty ditch for

"sunken treasure," hoping to find something of value that had dropped into the canal. If a little water remained, it would freeze and become a skating rink.

From Albany, some captains might have a steamboat pull them down the Hudson River to New York City to spend the winter. There, hundreds of canal boats would tie up side by side. Now that the kids were not traveling every day, they

CHILDREN WHO GREW UP ON CANAL BOATS

HAD AN EVER-CHANGING VIEW

OUT THEIR CABIN WINDOWS.

attended public schools. Sometimes while they were in class, their family's boat might be hired to do a small job. When kids got out of school, they might discover their home was not where they left it in the morning. But they could find it simply by asking the dockmaster. He kept track of where the different boats tied up. When the canal reopened in the spring, the kids left the public schools and returned to the school of experience offered by the canal.

Greeting friends on other boats and catching up on the "towpath news" helped maintain a feeling of community on the Erie Canal. Also, people entertained themselves with music, singing along with a fiddle, harmonica, or concertina, an instrument similar to a small accordion. They swapped stories and legends about the Erie. In one "whopper" of a tale, it was said a whale had toured the canal. In another, a towpath mule named Agnes was sold to a Virginia planter. Headstrong and stubborn, Agnes abandoned the plow and joined the horses on a fox hunt, where she jumped fences like a kangaroo and got to the fox before the hounds did.

And then there's the story of Joshua, a polliwog taken from the canal. He grew to be a hundred-year-old frog with legs six feet long. He set up residence in a pond in Empeyville, near Rome. He was such a giant that every time he jumped into the water, the splash rose 30 feet into the air, and the pond grew six feet wider.

Another popular story spread the fame of McCarthy, a legendary mule trainer. "Everybody" wanted to buy a mule from him. Supposedly he found a way to save time when mules were taken from the towpath at the end of their shift and loaded back onto the boat. Instead of lowering the "hoss-bridge" for the mules to cross on, McCarthy trained his mules to walk the tow rope like circus performers on a tightrope. Now *that* would be something to see-and good storytellers could almost convince their listeners that they had.

Children who grew up on canal boats had an ever-changing view out their cabin windows. But in the late 1850s, their world—always on the move—began to change in ways even the canallers could never have imagined. The heyday of the Grand Erie Canal was about to end.

Chapter Twelve

WHEELS OF PROGRESS

IN THE EARLY DAYS OF THE ERIE, WEALTHY westbound travelers who were in a hurry left Albany on expensive stagecoaches instead of on the canal. That way they avoided its first 24-mile stretch, which had 27 locks and took an entire day to get through. By coach, travelers could cover that distance in only three hours. Once in Schenectady, they would board a packet. From that point on, the canal provided a faster, more pleasant ride. In 1831, another option, even faster, became available—America's first steam railroad. On the train, the trip between Albany and Schenectady took only one hour. The name of the train was the *DeWitt Clinton*.

Railroads were first built in many short stretches. Because of the canal's long length, short rail lines offered

IN THE MIDDLE OF THE 19TH CENTURY, RAILROADS REPLACED THE ERIE CANAL FOR MOST PASSENGER TRAVEL.

little competition. Also, compared to the comfort and safety of packet boats, the first locomotives seemed dangerous, dirty, and unreliable. Their future was uncertain. When a locomotive was shipped on a canal boat in 1836 to Rochester for the Tonawanda Railroad, there was no cry of alarm. Nor were canallers worried when the first locomotive for the Auburn and Rochester Railroad came by canal boat in 1842.

As technology improved, the railroads grew safer and more dependable. And they were fast, sometimes traveling up to 20 miles per hour. Just as some people had objected to the "unnatural" speed of four miles an hour on the early canal boats, in the 1850s some called the trains' speed "ungodly." But most Americans loved going places fast, and many of them could not wait to try the "iron horse." Railroads caught on, and more tracks were laid, finally stretching all the way across the state. By 1860, a train ride between Albany and Buffalo took only a day. On the canal, the trip still took a week.

Rail owners took advantage of the fact that the canal closed during the winter. They cut passenger rates to almost nothing in the summer, so people could travel faster and cheaper by rail than by canal. Then the railroads charged high rates in the winter when they had no competition from the canal. The railroads still made a profit, and by 1860 almost all the packet boats had gone out of business. A few continued to take large groups on weekend excursions. And some mailboats had regular runs to deliver mail, packages,

THE *DEWITT CLINTON* STEAM LOCOMOTIVE

and an occasional passenger. However, the era of packet boat passenger travel had come to a close.

But the Erie still provided the best means of travel for heavy freight, for which speed was not an issue. Canal tolls were abolished in 1882. The canal had paid for itself more than 30 times over. It had cleared $42 million over and above its construction, enlargement, maintenance, and operation costs.

At the beginning of the 20th century, more than six million tons of freight were being shipped on the canal every year. If the canal were made wider and deeper, it could accommodate much larger boats called barges. Barges could carry as much as 500 tons of cargo, more than double the amount that canal boats were carrying in 1900. The main promoter of the idea to expand the canal was none other than

George Clinton, grandson of DeWitt Clinton. New York
governor Theodore Roosevelt, who later became the 26th
President of the United States, asked the federal government
to help fund the expansion. Just as had happened when the
original Erie Canal was built, the answer was no. Also once
again, the citizens of New York State said yes.

George Clinton was called the "Father of the Barge
Canal System." Costing 101 million dollars, the rebuilding
of the canal began in 1905. The project took 13 years. Much
of the original Erie was rerouted. Advanced engineering
allowed builders to make dams that "canalized" rivers
previously too rough for safe boating. The canal was
widened from 70 feet to 125 feet and deepened from 7 feet
to at least 12 feet. Locks were expanded to 300 feet long and
44½ feet wide. Towpaths were removed. No more would
mules, horses, or oxen pull boats along. They would be
propelled either by their own engines or by tugboats.

Although barges made up the bulk of the boats,
passenger craft still carried some travelers east and west.
For example, in 1910 a group of University of Rochester
students chartered a canal boat called the *Rambler*. They
cruised to Utica to cheer their football team to victory over
Hamilton College. Judging by the story told by one of the
fans, their novice efforts to maneuver the boat proved as
enjoyable as the football game. He said, "The Erie itself was
quiet and serene but what it failed to furnish in excitement
was supplied by the antics of the boat." It bumped into other

boats and the canal walls, which fortunately held up in spite of the young men's inexperienced steering.

For the entire Barge Canal System, bridges had a minimum clearance of 15½ feet. That's about twice as high as the bridges on the original Erie Canal. Because of the level of some roads crossing the Barge Canal System, designers chose to keep 16 of the bridges low. They are lift bridges that can be raised to allow boaters to pass.

But the era of low bridges was remembered fondly. In 1913, Thomas Allen published his song "Low Bridge, Everybody Down." It became a huge hit. Its refrain is still well known a century later.

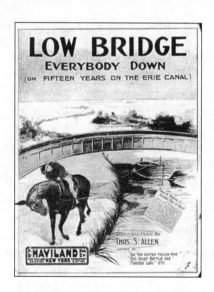

THE COVER FOR THE SHEET MUSIC FOR "LOW BRIDGE, EVERYBODY DOWN"

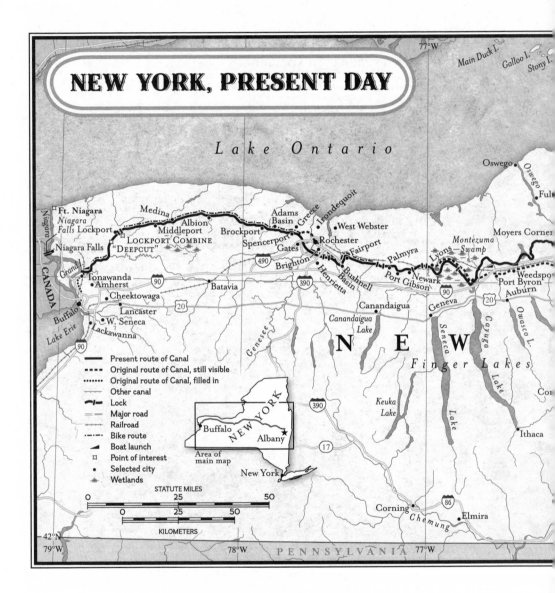

NEW YORK, PRESENT DAY

Lake Ontario

Main Duck I.   Galloo I.   Stony I.

Oswego   Oswego   Ful

Ft. Niagara   Medina   Adams   Greece   Irondequoit   West Webster   Moyers Corner
Niagara   Albion   Basin   Rochester   *Montezuma*
Falls Lockport   Middleport   Brockport   Fairport   Palmyra   — *Swamp*
LOCKPORT COMBINE   Spencerport   Lyons   Weedspo
"DEEPCUT"   Gates   Port Gibson   Newark   Port Byron
Niagara Falls   490   Brighton   Bushnell   Auburn
Grand I.   Basin
Tonawanda   90   Henrietta   Port Gibson   90   20
Amherst   Batavia   390   Geneva
Cheektowaga   Canandaigua
Lancaster   20   N   E   W
Buffalo   W. Seneca   *Canandaigua*
Lake Erie   Lackawanna   *Lake*   *Finger Lakes*   Co
90

Present route of Canal   *Genesee*   *Keuka*
Original route of Canal, still visible   *Lake*   Ithaca
Original route of Canal, filled in
Other canal   390
Lock
Major road   NEW YORK   17
Railroad   Buffalo
Bike route   Albany
Boat launch   Area of   86
□ Point of interest   main map   New York   Corning   *Chemung*   Elmira
• Selected city
⚲ Wetlands

STATUTE MILES
0   25   50

0   25   50
KILOMETERS

CANADA

42°N
79°W   78°W   P E N N S Y L V A N I A   77°W

77°W

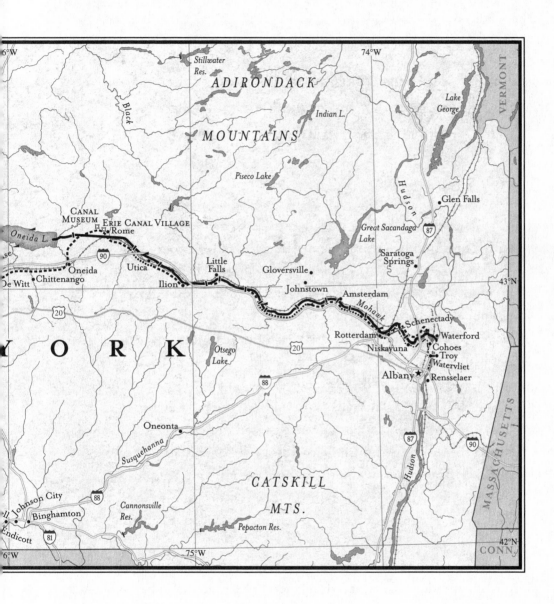

THE ERIE CANAL TODAY
IS A BUSY TRANSPORTATION CORRIDOR.

THE ERIE ITSELF WAS QUIET AND SERENE

BUT WHAT IT FAILED TO FURNISH IN EXCITEMENT WAS

SUPPLIED BY THE ANTICS OF THE BOAT.

By the middle of the 20th century, barges were still transporting more than five million tons of freight along the canal every year. Each barge could carry the equivalent cargo of 100 trucks or a 40-car train. But freight volume dropped off in the late 1950s to only 72,000 tons a year, largely because of competition from faster trucks, petroleum pipelines, railroads, and especially the St. Lawrence Seaway, which opened in 1958. It was developed on the St. Lawrence River in eastern Canada. Like the Erie, the St. Lawrence Seaway joins the Great Lakes, but the entrance to the Seaway from the Atlantic Ocean is closer to Europe. Also, it was built using more modern engineering techniques, so it is wider and deeper than the Erie and has fewer locks. Therefore it can handle larger commercial ships than the Erie can, and they can travel more quickly.

As use declined, the canal was neglected, but its impact was still evident. The canal defined the location of the state's major cities along the trade route it made possible between New York City and Buffalo. Nearly four of every

**A BOAT ENTERING A LOCK ON THE ST. LAWRENCE SEAWAY,
LARGER AND NEWER THAN THE ERIE CANAL**

five residents in upstate New York lived within 25 miles of
the Erie Canal.

For several decades, the canal was little used, but it would
not be forgotten.

Chapter Thirteen

LET'S CRUISE

MOST OF THE TRAFFIC ON THE ERIE Canal today is recreational. The variety of boats plying its waters includes oceangoing yachts en route between the Great Lakes and the Atlantic, crew shells, motorboats, fishing boats, canoes, and kayaks. Cities and towns have created canal-side parks that provide plenty of room for boats to tie up for a quick visit or an overnight stay.

Like vacationers traveling in RVs on land, each evening families and friends cruising the Erie on a houseboat come to these parks and plug in their electrical cords and water hoses. Most towns provide picnic sites and barbecues, and many offer shower facilities. Businesses encourage boaters to shop, dine, visit a local museum, take a bike ride along the towpath, or just do the laundry while they're in town. Many

ACCUSTOMED TO THE BOATS, MALLARD DUCKS AND OTHER WILDLIFE FLOURISH ON THE CANAL.

towns stage annual Canalfests featuring live music, arts and crafts, food, dancing, and amusement-park rides. Historic reenactments and boat parades are regularly scheduled.

Today's Erie Canal has 57 locks. More than 100,000 boats pass through them each year. The electric-powered, 32-ton lock gates open and close in 30 seconds. Locks raise or lower boats in 10 to 30 minutes, depending on the height of the lock. Locks operate daily from seven in the morning until ten at night, the longest working day of any canal in

A SUMMER CONCERT AT A PAVILION ON THE ERIE CANAL IN AMSTERDAM, NEW YORK

A PASSENGER BOAT ENTERS A LOCK.

the country. Weather permitting, the canal opens the first
Monday in May and remains open until mid-November.
Maintenance is done during the winter months when the
canal is partially drained. Huge solid-steel guard gates
about every ten miles along the canal can be lowered to close
portions of the canal for repair work or to prevent damage
in case of a break in a canal wall.

In December 2000, the federal government designated
the Erie and its connecting canals as the Erie Canalway
National Heritage Corridor in order to protect and promote
the canals themselves, their history, and the recreational
opportunities they provide. Now the nation, not just the

BOATS TIED UP IN FAIRPORT, A VILLAGE EAST OF ROCHESTER THAT IS
SOMETIMES CALLED THE "CROWN JEWEL" OF THE ERIE CANAL

state of New York, is committed to preserving the landmark
that began as "Clinton's Ditch."

Over the years, the Erie Canal has meant many things
to many people. To Jesse Hawley in a Canandaigua jail
cell, the canal promised a way for merchants to ship their
goods. For the engineers and laborers who built the canal,
completing America's most ambitious public works project
was a challenge they were proud to meet. For immigrants,
the canal offered a route to better lives. For DeWitt Clinton,
it was the means of transforming New York into the Empire
State, the leader of the nation in the number and diversity
of its residents, as well as in technology, engineering, and

transportation. The canal helped the United States fulfill its potential, carrying goods, people, and ideas between the heart of America and the rest of the world.

Nearly two centuries have passed since the Wedding of the Waters, yet the story of the grand Erie Canal continues to inspire. It shows what is possible with a "can-do" attitude, an American spirit valued as much today as it was when the Ditch was dug.

STATUE OF A HOGGEE AND A MULE, A LANDMARK IN SYRACUSE

CHRONOLOGY

1807-1808 Grain merchant Jesse Hawley publishes articles describing
how a canal might be built between the Hudson River
and Lake Erie.

1812-1815 War of 1812 against Great Britain

1817 DeWitt Clinton takes office as governor of New York State.

1817 Erie Canal building begins.

1819 The first section of the canal, 16 miles long, opens for use.

1820 Another 73 miles of the canal are opened, and population growth
makes New York the largest state in the nation.

1825 The completed Erie Canal opens.

1828 Governor DeWitt Clinton, the Father of the Erie Canal, dies.

1836 Work begins to enlarge the Erie Canal.

1862 The enlargement is completed. The Erie's width increases from
40 feet to 75 feet and its depth from 4 feet to 7 feet.

1882 Tolls are abolished. The canal has earned $42 million over and
above the original cost to build it, as well as the cost to maintain
and enlarge it.

1903 Work begins to enlarge the Erie again as part of the New York
State Barge Canal System.

1918 The enlargement is completed. The Erie's width increases
generally to 200 feet and the depth to a minimum of 12 feet.

2000 The federal government establishes the Erie Canalway National
Heritage Corridor.

GLOSSARY

AQUEDUCT
A bridge that carries water.

BILGE
The lowest part of a boat, where water collects.

ESCARPMENT
A large rock cliff.

HOGGEE (HOAG-gee)
The person who led and cared for the mules who pulled boats on the 19th Century Erie Canal, typically a boy 10 to 15 years old.

LOCK
On a canal or river, a chamber with gates on both ends. Boats enter the lock from one level of the canal or river, and then water is drained in or out of the lock in order to raise or lower the boat to the level of water in the next section of the waterway.

MORTAR
The cement-like material that fills the gaps between stones or bricks in a wall.

SLUICE
A man-made channel designed for carrying water.

TINKER
A traveling repairman who mends kitchen or household utensils.

WEIGH LOCK
A lock in which boats can be weighed, empty or loaded, usually for determining the fees they must pay for the amount of cargo they are carrying.

A HISTORIC POSTCARD

RESOURCES

AUTHOR'S BIBLIOGRAPHY

Adams, Samuel Hopkins. *The Erie Canal.* Random House, 1953.

Bernstein, Peter L. *Wedding of the Waters; The Erie Canal and the Making of a Great Nation.* Norton, 2005.

Finch, Roy G. *The Story of the New York State Canals: Historical and Commercial Information.* State Engineer and Surveyor, State of New York, 1925.

Hosack, David. *Memoir of DeWitt Clinton: With an Appendix, Containing Numerous Documents, Illustrative of the Principal Events of His Life.* J. Seymour, 1829. Available at www.history.rochester.edu/canal/bib/hosack/Contents.html.

Merrill, Arch. *The Towpath.* Empire State Books, 1989, originally published in 1945.

Rapp, Marvin A. *Canal Water and Whiskey.* Heritage Press, 1992.

Rutherford, John. *Facts and Observations in Relation to the Origin and Completion of the Erie Canal.* N.B. Holmes, 1825. Available at www.history.rochester.edu/canal/bib/rutherford/fact1825.htm.

Shaw, Ronald E. *Erie Water West: A History of the Erie Canal, 1792-1854.* University of Kentucky Press, 1966.

Sheriff, Carol. *The Artificial River: The Erie Canal and the Paradox of Progress, 1817-1862.* Hill and Wang, 1996.

FIND OUT MORE

BOOKS

Hullfish, William. *The Canaller's Songbook.* American Canal and Transportation Center, 1984.

Levy, Janey. *Erie Canal: A Primary Source History of the Canal That Changed America.* Rosen, 2003.

Lourie, Peter. *Erie Canal: Canoeing America's Great Waterway.* Boyds Mills Press, 1997.

Myers, Anna. *Hoggee.* Walker, 2004.

Panagopoulos, Janie Lynn. *Erie Trail West.* River Road Press, 1995.

Rossi, Louis, *Cycling along the Canals of New York.* Vitesse Press, 2006.

Stack, Debbie J., and Donald A. Wilson, editors. *Always Know Your Pal: Children on the Erie Canal.* Erie Canal Museum, 1993.

Wyld, Lionel D. *Low Bridge! Folklore and the Erie Canal.* Syracuse University Press, 1962.

ILLUSTRATIONS CREDITS

WEBSITES

http://www.canals.state.ny.us
Information on the New York State canals today

http://www.eriecanal.org
Information about the Erie Canal and links to many other sites

http://www.eriecanalmuseum.org
The Erie Canal Museum in Syracuse, New York, with links to other canal museum web sites.

www.eriecanalvillage.org
You can find the lyrics for the song "Low Bridge, Everybody Down" at this site.

http://www.nycanaltimes.com
A statewide canal online newspaper

PLACES TO VISIT

The Erie Canal Museum
318 Erie Blvd East
Syracuse, NY 13202

The Erie Canal Village
5789 New London Road
Rome, NY 13440

GC = The Granger Collection, New York; NYHS = Collection of the New-York Historical Society; BAL = The Bridgeman Art Library; ECM = The Erie Canal Museum, Syracuse, NY www.eriecanalmuseum.org; FES = Frank E. Sadowski Jr., *Erie Canal,* http://www.eriecanal.org;

Front Cover: © NYHS, USA/BAL. Back Cover: GC; 1 Title Page, GC; 6,© North Wind Picture Archives/Alamy; 8, Hulton Archive/Getty Images; 9,Library of Congress, Prints and Photographs Division, LC-USZ62-43549; 10–11, Justin Morrill, The M Factory; 14, GC; 17, GC; 18, GC; 20–21, © Museum of the City of New York, USA/BAL; 23, GC; 24, © Stock Montage, Inc./Alamy; 27, © Classic Image/Alamy; 30, Service Historique de la Marine, Vincennes, France, Archives Charmet/BAL; 32, GC; 34, GC; 37, Courtesy ECM; 38, GC; 40, © NYHS, USA/BAL; 45, © Bettmann/CORBIS; 46, GC; 47, © North Wind Picture Archives/Alamy; 48, GC; 49, Masterfile Royalty Free; 50, © NYHS, USA/BAL; 52, Stuart Armstrong/GC; 53, © The Image Works Archives; 55, © Museum of the City of New York/CORBIS; 59, Department of Rare Books and Special Collections, University of Rochester Libraries; 60, © North Wind Picture Archives/Alamy; 64, © CORBIS; 65, GC; 66–67, Justin Morrill, The M Factory adapted from "Map of the Canal, and Profile of the Canal" — from: *Marco Paul's Voyages & Travels, Erie Canal,*by Jacob Abbott. (Harper & Brothers, New York, c1852) — frontispiece; 68, GC; 70, FES; 73, wrmgraphics.com; 74–75, Albany Institute of History & Art; 78, Private Collection, The Stapleton Collection/BAL; 80, © North Wind Picture Archives/Alamy; 83, GC; 85, ©The Image Works Archives; 86, The New York Public Library/Art Resource, NY; 88, © The Mariners' Museum/CORBIS; 90, GC; 91, FES; 92, © North Wind Pictures; 94, © Roger-Viollet/The Image Works; 94, The Art Archive/Gift of the Coe Foundation/Buffalo Bill Historical Center, Cody, Wyoming/23.67; 96, GC; 98, GC; 100, Image courtesy of ECM; 100, akg-images, London; 103, Private Collection,/BAL; 103, © Peabody Essex Museum, Salem, Massachusetts, USA/BAL; 103, GC; 106, Art Resource, NY; 109, GC; 111, image courtesy of New York State Canal Corporation; 112–113, Justin Morrill, M Factory; 115, © William A. Bake/CORBIS; 116, © Doug Wilson/Alamy; 118, ©Mitch Wojnarowicz/Amsterdam Recorder/The Image Works; 119, ABC Creative Group, courtesy of Mid-Lakes Navigation Company; 119, © Joseph Sohm/Visions of America/Corbis; 120, © Peter Steiner/Alamy; 121, Courtesy ECM; 123, FES

INDEX

Founded in 1888, the National
Geographic Society is one of the
largest nonprofit scientific and
educational organizations in the
world. It reaches more than 285
million people worldwide each
month through its official journal,
NATIONAL GEOGRAPHIC, and its four
other magazines; the National
Geographic Channel; television
documentaries; radio programs;
films; books; videos and DVDs;
maps; and interactive media.
National Geographic has funded
more than 8,000 scientific
research projects and supports
an education program combating
geographic illiteracy.

For more information, please call
1-800-NGS LINE (647-5463)
or write to the following address:

NATIONAL GEOGRAPHIC SOCIETY
1145 17th Street N.W., Washington,
D.C. 20036-4688 U.S.A.

Visit us online at
www.nationalgeographic.com/books

*For information about special
discounts for bulk purchases, please contact*
National Geographic Books Special
Sales: ngspecsales@ngs.org

*For rights or permissions inquiries,
please contact* National Geographic
Books Subsidiary Rights:
ngbookrights@ngs.org